The Seceders

D0784927

The Seceders

The Story of J. C. Philpot and William Tiptaft

J. H. PHILPOT, MD

'In all things approving ourselves as the ministers of God' [2 Cor. 6:4]

The Banner of Truth Trust
78b Chiltern Street, London, W1

THE FOLLOWING PAGES ARE, WITH CONSIDERABLE RE-arrangement and necessary adjustments, extracted from *The Seceders* (1829–69), volumes I and II, first published 1930–32. These two volumes, consisting mainly of the letters of J. C. Philpot and William Tiptaft, are both prefaced with a biographical introduction by Dr J. H. Philpot as a background to the letters. It is this introduction, augmented in places with extracts from the letters, which is here reprinted. A third volume of *The Seceders* containing Philpot's letters from 1850 to his death, with an introduction by S. F. Paul of Brighton, was published in 1960, but as this reprint concentrates on the early ministries of these men, only minor use has been made of it. We would like to record the help given in the preparation of this edition by S. F. Paul and J. H. Gosden, Editor of the *Gospel Standard*, and also the co-operation of the Aged Pilgrims' Friend Society, further notice of which will be found on page 205.

Printed in Great Britain by
Billing & Sons Ltd.,
Guildford & London

Contents

The Philpot and Tiptaft families

PHILPOT

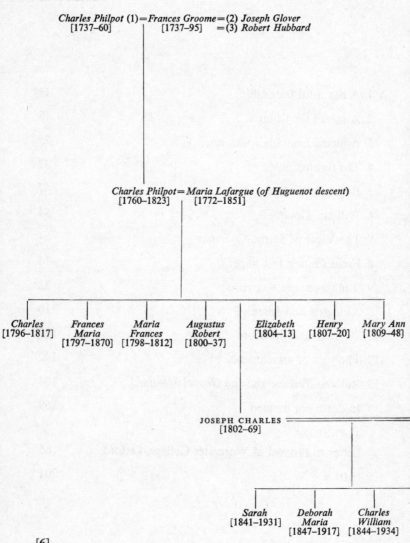

Charles Philpot (1) = Frances Groome = (2) Joseph Glover
[1737–60]   [1737–95]   = (3) Robert Hubbard

Charles Philpot = Maria Lafargue (*of Huguenot descent*)
[1760–1823]   [1772–1851]

Charles [1796–1817] Frances Maria [1797–1870] Maria Frances [1798–1812] Augustus Robert [1800–37] Elizabeth [1804–13] Henry [1807–20] Mary Ann [1809–48]

JOSEPH CHARLES [1802–69]

Sarah [1841–1931] Deborah Maria [1847–1917] Charles William [1844–1934]

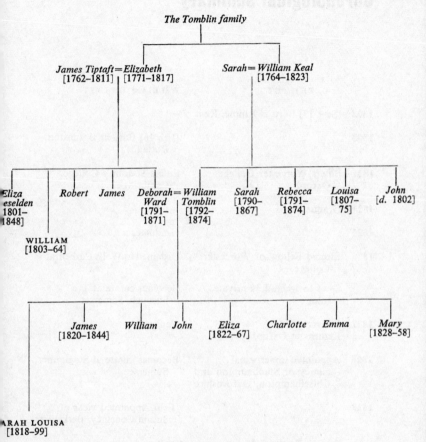

The Tomblin family

James Tiptaft=Elizabeth
[1762–1811] [1771–1817]

Sarah=William Keal
[1764–1823]

Eliza eselden 1801–1848]

Robert   *James*

Deborah=William *Ward* *Tomblin* [1791– [1792– 1871] 1874]

Sarah [1790– 1867]

Rebecca [1791– 1874]

Louisa [1807– 75]

John [d. 1802]

WILLIAM [1803–64]

James [1820–1844]

William   *John*

Eliza [1822–67]

Charlotte   *Emma*

Mary [1828–58]

ARAH LOUISA [1818–99]

Joseph Henry [1850–1940]

[7]

Chronological Summary

	J. C. PHILPOT	WILLIAM TIPTAFT
1802	[Sept 13] Born at Ripple, Kent	
1803		[Feb 16] Born at Braunston, Rutland
1821	Enters Worcester College, Oxford	Enters St John's College, Cambridge
1824	Graduates B.A.	
1825		Graduates B.A.
1826	Elected Fellow of Worcester College	Ordained in Wells Cathedral
	Goes to Ireland as private tutor	Becomes curate at Treborough, Somerset
1827	Converted Returns to Oxford	Converted
1828	Appointed to perpetual curacy of Stadhampton and Chiselhampton, Oxfordshire	Becomes curate at Stogumber, Somerset
1829		[Feb] Appointed vicar of Sutton Courtney, Berkshire
	[June] First meeting of Philpot and Tiptaft	
1831		[Nov] Leaves the Church of England
1832		[March] New chapel at Abingdon opened
		[June] Baptized at Devizes

J. C. PHILPOT	WILLIAM TIPTAFT
1835 [March] Leaves the Church of England	
Resigns his College Fellowship	
[Sept] Baptized at Allington, Wilts	
1837 Publishes two sermons: 'Heir of Heaven' and 'Winter afore Harvest'	
1838 Marries Sarah Keal of Oakham	
Accepts joint pastorate at Oakham and Stamford	
1843	Forms Strict Baptist Church at Abingdon
1849 Becomes sole editor of *Gospel Standard*	
1864	[Aug] Dies at Abingdon
[Oct] Resigns pastorate at Oakham and Stamford	
1869 Dies at Croydon	

1: A beautiful friendship

IN THE FRUITFUL VALE OF BERKS, AMID A MAZE OF lanes and by-roads, near the edge of the downs and only a mile or two south of the spot where wicked men have planted Didcot Junction, lies the ancient village of East Hagbourne, with its late-Norman Church, its half-timbered cottages, its old wayside praying-cross, and its big yews clipped into the semblance of beehives. In such a setting just a hundred years ago – in July 1829, to be precise – at a clerical gathering held in its pleasant vicarage, two earnest young clergymen, neither of whom had yet completed his twenty-seventh year, happened to meet, practically for the first time, and then and there to lay the foundations of a friendship, of which it might be said, as of a happy marriage, that it had been veritably made in heaven, because each brought to it gifts which the other needed. One, the younger by five months, had come over on foot from his newly-furnished vicarage at Sutton Courtney, a large and at that time unadvertised village on the Isis, as the Thames above Dorchester was then locally called, to which living he had been presented no longer back than the previous February by the Dean and Canons of Windsor. But the other, having still more recently vacated his stately rooms in Worcester College, Oxford, of which, however, he still remained a Fellow, had had a ten-mile ride across country and river from his cheerless lodgings on the green at Stadhampton, a remote, unhealthy village in the waterlogged valley of the Thame, of which he had held the Perpetual Curacy for something over a year.

In the course of that summer afternoon, weary, perhaps of discussing the burning question of the day, Catholic Emancipation, they drew apart from the others and paced the vicarage garden side by side, diving into each other's minds and hearts. And they could no more have told whither, under Providence, their new intimacy was to lead them, than the impetuous Isis and the pensive Thame, when they join streams by Dorchester meadows, can foresee the Essex Flats.

Thirty years later, after they had long since passed through their days of storm and stress, and each had found a peaceful, if obscure retreat, I knew them both as intimately as a child can know his elders, for one was my father, Joseph Charles Philpot, of blessed memory, and the other, no whit less worthy of enduring affection and esteem, was my mother's uncle, William Tiptaft, of St John's College, Cambridge.

Despised and 'disallowed indeed of men', self-separated as far as is humanly possible from a hostile world, following Christ, to quote my father, 'not in respectability and honour, with maces and organs and greetings in the market-place, and "Rabbi, Rabbi," but in contempt and shame', they were nevertheless fashioned, I venture to claim, on the pattern of the prophets and the saints of old, who also had no honour in their own time and tribe, because they would not bow down to the idols of the day. They had given up almost everything men value for what they felt to be the truth, and like all who are guided by the Holy Spirit in the footsteps of their Lord, they had their full share of trials and afflictions, of doubts and misgivings. Yet had they their recompense. For, as my father was able to affirm out of a long experience, 'the life of faith is the most blessed that a man can lead upon earth'. They cherished no vague, sentimental yearnings after the bygone Ages of Faith. They lived and moved in one, surrounded by their humble but devoted followers.

Seen through the haze of sixty years, their lives read like a romance. Alongside their willing descent into obscurity, biographies of successful climbers, of aspiring churchmen even, and others, who have helped themselves to fame, leave me lukewarm, for the secret of romance lies, not in success, but in self-sacrifice. And yet outside their own connection their names are scarcely known. You will search for them in vain in the hospitable pages of the *Dictionary of National Biography*. Their story has never been properly told, still less advertised, nor that of the obscure religious revival in which they played a leading part. Told it will certainly some day be, though it may have to wait for a century or two and an abler pen than mine, when it will naturally fall into its appointed niche in the religious record of the nineteenth century. For, when faithfully recorded, authentic spiritual experience, such as miraculously changes a man's whole purpose in life, has a perennial value and, in the long run, an astonishingly wide appeal.

*

To me with my four-score years it is no great effort to carry my mind back to that critical July afternoon a century ago, and to visualize the two ardent young seekers after truth pacing the vicarage lawn in their formal clerical garb of tall silk hats, black broad-cloth coats with wide, high roll-collars, soft white pleated shirtfronts, their necks imprisoned up to their jaws in high stocks and snowy cravats, their tight black trousers kept in place securely by riding-straps passed under their Oxford shoes.

Both are good-looking men, my father remarkably so. He is the taller and evidently the less robust and active of the two, with the stoop of one who has pored much over the lamp-lit book, and whose chest is not too strong. His fine, dark, impressive eyes, inherited from his Huguenot mother, and the high fixed colour over the cheek-bones—ruddy, like young David's

—also hint at some delicacy of constitution. When for a moment he takes off his hat to wipe his moist brow with a large bandanna handkerchief, his straight raven-black hair is seen to be brushed in a smooth wide band across a pale fore-head, which is broad rather than high. Indeed, neither he nor his new acquaintance can boast of the poet's domed head. His movements are rather languid, not full of breezy life like those of his companion, who has on this occasion to bridle his pace to the other's more measured and meditative tread. For usually the young Vicar of Sutton Courtney is one who walks about most briskly on his Master's business and wastes no time in futile speculation. He is a very earnest, active Christian, and some day his overflowing energy will wear him out. He comes of an old stock, which, through generations of work upon the land as yeoman farmers, has yet retained the delicate aquiline features of a remoter ancestry. He has a squarish head, a pale face, grey eyes, fine silky light-brown hair, and the look of one who loves his fellow-men.

'About this time,' to quote my father's record of their first encounter, 'I belonged to what is called a clerical meeting, a few of the evangelical clergy of the neighbourhood meeting together once a month at each other's houses for the purpose of reading the Bible, prayer and religious conversation. Some time in May 1829[1] I was present at one of these assemblings, I think, if I remember right, at Wallingford, and there for the first time I met William Tiptaft, who had lately joined. He, as being a stranger, said little at the meeting, nor did we come at all close together. We met, however, again early in the same summer at another clerical meeting at Hagbourne, near Sutton Courtney, and there, as we were walking out for a little air, after the main

---

[1] From a letter of William Tiptaft's, on whom this first meeting seems to have made a deep impression, we learn that it really took place 'at Mr. Langley's, Wallingford', on 11 June 1829.

business of the day was over, he drew near and began to converse on the things of God. At that time I was further advanced, at least in doctrine and a knowledge of the letter of truth, than he was, being a firm believer in election and the distinguishing doctrines of sovereign grace, which I preached according to the ability that God gave. We therefore soon got on the topic of election, when I at once perceived that he had not been led into the grand truths of the gospel, and though not altogether opposed to them, yet like many others in his state, viewed them with a measure of both fear and suspicion. I was struck, however, even then with his great sincerity of spirit and the thoroughly practical view which he seemed to take upon all matters of religion, considering them, as he always did so markedly through the whole of his subsequent life, as the great, the all-important, the one thing needful for time and eternity.'[1]

In this encounter, it may be worth noting, it was the new Vicar of Sutton Courtney who made the first advances. It was characteristic of him, for he was a very friendly and forthcoming person, much more so than my father, who was naturally reserved and not very easy to know. In fact, to use the current phrase, William Tiptaft was a typical extrovert, showing his emotions vividly upon his face, talking and gesticulating freely and easily, and soon striking up a friendship with those to whom he was drawn. He was naïve, fervid and trenchantly sincere, though neither highly intellectual nor fond of books. Even later on, if one may be forgiven the misquotation, 'his studie was on litel *but* the Bible'. Newspapers he systematically banned, as inventions of the Evil One, and who shall say that some are not?

There is a passage in one of my father's Reviews, contrasting the two great Genevan Reformers, John Calvin and William

[1] Philpot, J. C. *Memoir of William Tiptaft*. (London, 1867), p. 17.

Farel, which might have been written of himself and his new friend in their subsequent relations, and which may be here conveniently quoted, before we pass on, or rather go back, to consider their parentage, and what in a medical casebook would be termed their 'previous history':

'As coadjutors Calvin and Farel were admirably mated. Farel was a man of action, Calvin a man of thought; Farel was a preacher of fiery eloquence, Calvin a writer of deep but calm Scriptural knowledge. Both were ardent lovers of truth, bosom friends and affectionate brethren for life, and so matched as fellow-labourers, that Farel's impetuosity urged on Calvin's slowness, and Calvin's judgment restrained Farel's rashness.'[1]

While my father, for instance, always distrusted 'enthusiasm', false fire, and the wide-flung net, and preferred to preach to those who had already been converted (in many cases by his friend), William Tiptaft had in him much of the revivalist. The fact that so few men were really 'troubled by their sins' was to him a perpetual grief. To the end of his days he continued to call men to repentance in a loud and resonant voice which could fill the largest building, shaking his head, twisting one white hand upon the other, and bringing out his curt sentences slowly and deliberately, with pauses between, as if he had been driving in a heavy nail. 'A little time will sweep us all into the grave, and where will our souls be? We are fit to die, or we are not. Is my soul quickened? Am I born again? Are my sins pardoned? What is my real state before God?' and so on. The effect of this impassioned iteration would have been only impaired by any intrusion of doctrinal dialectic. 'The Gospel of the grace of God', wrote my father, 'is not a thing to be proved, but a truth to be believed. It is not submitted to our reasoning powers, as a subject for critical examination, but is

[1] Philpot, J. C. *Reviews* (Reprinted from the Gospel Standard) Vol. I (London, 1901), p. 595.

a message from God, addressed to our conscience, feelings and affections. For this reason men fond of argument and proving everything by strictly logical deduction generally make very poor preachers.' 'In the Scriptures,' he says elsewhere, 'God does not argue.' An august example!

2: A son of the Church

EARLY IN 1760, OR POSSIBLY IN THE PREVIOUS autumn, a good-looking young couple, neither of them many months older than the promising youth who was soon to ascend the British throne as George III, were married at Leicester. Their names were Charles Philpot and Frances Groome. The former, to judge from the pencil sketch in my possession, was a dapper, delicate-featured youth, with a good brow and sensitive lips; the bride, even in the oil portrait taken in later years, shows signs of having possessed considerable beauty. Of Charles Philpot little is known, except that he came from Lewes, played the harpsichord, and was possibly a teacher of music, for time was not vouchsafed him in which to show his quality. Some illness carried him off at the early age of twenty-three, and on 4 August 1760, two days after his death, he was buried in the graveyard of St Martin's, Leicester, leaving his young widow to bear the consequences of their somewhat improvident union. The man-child, born after his death and baptized by his name, was my grandfather, Charles Philpot.

A few years later Frances Groome had the good fortune to find an excellent second husband in a worthy Leicestershire yeoman, named Joseph Glover, who, as the marriage proved childless, most ably and willingly devoted all his care to bringing up his promising young stepson, with an affection for which that same stepson never ceased to be grateful.

At that date the Wyggeston Free Grammar School at Leicester, under the able headmastership of the Rev. Gerard Andrewes, had achieved a high repute for the fine classical scholars it turned out, the most distinguished of whom was that 'noted oddity, the Rev. Richard Farmer, D.D., a pioneer in Shakespearean exegesis and eventually Master of Emmanuel College, Cambridge. It was due to him, I believe, that young Charles Philpot, when the time came for him to go up to the University, after as a day-boy he had learnt all that the Grammar School could teach him, chose Emmanuel for his College, made friends with many other scholars as eager as himself, and had his mind turned towards what was to be the rather fruitless hobby of his life, historical research. Joseph Glover, having seen his young stepson through the critical years of adolescence, died in 1778, leaving behind him such a fragrant memory that my grandfather, when he came to have children of his own, named his third son, my father, after him.

Frances Groome did not long remain a widow, and this time, as if to make up for her early struggles and privations, she found a rich husband in Robert Hubbard, a prominent Leicester solicitor, who had a daughter, Harriet, by a previous marriage, and who happened to be legal adviser to Rev. Peter Lafargue, of Stamford. By this time Charles Philpot was a promising young curate and private chaplain to the Earl of Harborough, and, living as at times he did under the same roof, he was naturally thrown much into the company of Miss Harriet Hubbard. It became the fond wish of both parents that their respective stepchildren should marry, and keep the money in the family. But, of course, it fell out otherwise, thanks chiefly to that exuberant young couple, the son and daughter of Peter Lafargue. Charles Philpot, the staid Anglo-Saxon, fell before the lively, exotic charm of the dark-eyed Maria Lafargue, while her brother, Peter Augustus, a dashing young cavalry subaltern, carried off the more homely Miss Hubbard and her handsome fortune.

Stamford, where Maria Lafargue lived with her father, step-mother, and two brothers before her marriage, strangely enough was later to be for over a quarter of a century the scene of my father's labours. William Wilberforce, passing through one Sunday in 1798, could find nothing better to say for it than 'This seems a sad, careless place. At Church, miserable work! Remnant of Sunday-school – eight children! I have never seen a more apparently irreligious place. A shopkeeper said none of the clergy were active, or went among the poor.' Perhaps, if good Mr Wilberforce could have found time to call on Peter Lafargue in that fine old freestone corner-house facing All Saints Church, which I remember being demolished, he might have modified his opinion.

My grandmother, Maria, had been born into the Church of England, in what you might even call its upper crust, for her maternal grandfather, a Russell, had once held the richest living in England, Doddington, in the Isle of Ely, worth over £7,000 a year, while Peter Lafargue, her father, and himself the son of a clergyman, having married two heiresses in succession, was quite well enough off to leave the loaves and fishes of preferment to those who stood in direr need of them. She was connected, moreover, with several high ecclesiastical dignitaries, and even through her stepmother, a niece of the Earl of Harborough (for her own mother had died in a decline when barely out of her teens), with that promising youth, E. B. Pusey,[1] who was to be ordained at the same time and by the same hands as my father.

It was on 24 July 1794 that she was eventually married to the Rev. Charles Philpot. Almost exactly a century earlier, toward the end of 1692, there had landed on these happy shores, after incredible afflictions, a young widow of twenty-eight, with a two-year-old baby in her arms. Her name was

---

[1] E. B. Pusey (1800–82), Regius Professor of Hebrew at Oxford, was, along with J. H. Newman, the foremost leader in the Oxford Movement.

Lidie Grenouilleau de Lafargue, and the baby, her little Élie, the sole survivor of her four children, was destined in due time to be Maria Lafargue's grandfather. She knew no English, but her dead husband's elder brother, Dr Jean de Lafargue, had been in this country since 1688, and money had been invested in her name in British funds. A century was to elapse, however, before her heirs and those of her dead husband could establish their claim to the property sequestrated on her flight.

The details of her pitiable story, unknown to my father, but since established through the indefatigable researches on the spot of the late Miss Ida Layard, his distant cousin, have been published in the *Proceedings of the Huguenot Society of London*, Vol. VII, 'Annals of a Quiet Family', and can only be summarized here. Her significance will appear as we proceed.

On 12 November 1684, just eleven months before a misguided France, by revoking the Edict of Nantes and declaring war to the death upon its Protestant subjects, wilfully threw overboard or, rather, transferred to its rivals, a ballast it could ill spare, a young advocate of twenty-four, named Samuel de Lafargue, was solemnly married in the Huguenot Temple of Castillon to Lidie Grenouilleau, a girl of twenty, whose father had also been an advocate. The bridegroom's parents both belonged to families of the old *noblesse*, which for generations had been faithful to the Huguenot cause. His father, old Samuel de Lafargue, who was an elder of his church, had the right to surmount his coat of arms with the empty helmet of a Count, while he himself bore the no less empty title of *Conseiller et Médecin du Roi*. The marriage was one of the last to be celebrated in the Castillon Temple, for only a year later it was closed and razed to the ground. During the troubled years 1686–90 four children were born to the young married couple,

[21]

of whom only one, the little Élie, eventually survived. Meanwhile the persecution raged, no mercy being shown either to rank or age. Old Samuel de Lafargue and his wife, too old to face the hazards of flight, were compelled to abjure, and shortly died and, after receiving 'the sacraments of penitence', were buried in consecrated ground, their own cemetery having been closed. Young Samuel held out until 1692, when he too was forced to abjure. As often happened, he died very soon after, and on the second birthday of his little Élie was buried beside his parents. There was nothing now to keep his young widow in Castillon. In daily agony lest her sole remaining child should be torn from her arms and brought up a Catholic, as had happened to the children of her friends, she faced intrepidly all the perils of flight, after she had shed her farewell tears over the many graves she would never set eyes on again. After forty years of widowhood, solaced by many friends of her own rank and religion, she makes her will (10 May 1732) 'after having entreated God to pardon all her sins in consideration of the Precious Blood of Jesus Christ, my Saviour and Redeemer'.

Meanwhile her little Élie has become the Rev. Elias Lafargue, M.A., of Clare College, Cambridge, and Rector of one of the pleasantest livings near Stamford, though rather too near the Fens, that of Gretford on the little river Glen. He remains a somewhat shadowy figure, who marries when he is thirty-four, has at the age of forty-seven an only son, Peter, and dies when he is sixty-three, leaving his widow well provided for, with 'chariot, chaise and horses', etc. The most vital thing he ever did for his progeny was to marry the grand-daughter of a notable *persecuté*, Pierre Samson de Cahanel of St Lô in the Côtentin, and thus to temper the warm Gascon blood of the Lafargues with a dour Norman element.

Now the whole point which these, perhaps tiresome, ancestral details are meant to lead up to is this, that the Rev. Peter

Lafargue, the only son of Elias and his French wife, had not a single drop of English blood in his veins, and that his daughter Maria, like the Newman brothers, whom we shall meet later on, might be fairly described as quite half a Huguenot. It was from her, beyond a doubt, and not from the placid Rector of Ripple, that my father derived his most salient characteristics, his warm and sensitive temperament, his firm and passionate devotion to truth, his gift of speech, restrained as it always was by a peculiarly French lucidity of thought and orderliness of presentment, and lastly his fresh complexion, his coal-black hair and his wonderful eyes. No pure-bred Anglo-Saxon ever looked out upon the world with eyes like his, large, luminous eyes, which could flash and lower and blaze and melt, and in fact do anything but twinkle.

The Rev. Charles Philpot and Maria his wife had eight children, no unusual family in those days, but only two of each sex succeeded in arriving at full maturity. The seeds of consumption found their way into that pleasant rectory and filled it with sorrow and apprehension. Between his eighth and his eighteenth year my father saw four of his young housemates, including his midshipman brother, carried to their graves in Ripple churchyard, in full view of the rectory windows, and who shall say with what terrors of death and judgment it must have filled his impressionable soul? The same thing was happening among his young cousins, the children of Colonel Lafargue. Few, indeed, of the crowded nurseries of that date were without their vacant chairs. 'Oh! say not thou that the former days were better than these!'

To his brother Henry, his junior by some four years, my father was warmly attached, and he felt his death at the age of thirteen acutely, hastened presumably as it had been by the brutality of his schoolmates, who turned the ailing child out of his bed one night and made him lie for hours on a bare stone floor. Such, at least, is my memory of what I heard from my father's lips.

As for my grandfather, his hobby was historical research, and after he had attended to his parish duties and set his children their lessons, he spent his ample leisure, as I am spending mine, with a pen in his hand and books at his elbow, thoroughly enjoying himself, no doubt, as he elaborated his Johnsonian antitheses. All that he succeeded in publishing, and that anonymously, was *A Literary History of the 14th and 15th Centuries*, which shows an enquiring mind and immense research, but he was, I believe, a frequent contributor to the *Gentleman's Magazine*, which in due course rewarded him with a handsome obituary. Now and again, as a holiday for himself and still more for his children, he would take coach to town with a £50 note in his pocket, to meet his learned friends and rummage in the public libraries, returning when his purse was empty and his notebooks full. His tastes, indeed, were rather literary than clerical, and, though he neglected no parish duty, religion seems to have sat upon him lightly, for my father tells us that until he went up to Oxford in 1821 he 'actually never knew that there was any such thing as religion professed beyond the mere Church of England formalism'.

3: Afflicted from his youth up

THE RECTORY OF RIPPLE — DELIGHTFUL NAME! — WHERE
my father first saw the light on 13 September 1802 lies in a shady
oasis on the bare chalk uplands a mile or two inland from Walmer, Deal, and the coast of Kent. The church has been rebuilt
since that date, and only the two centuries-old yews remain to
stand sentinel over the new-made[1] grave of John French, 1st
Earl of Ypres, of Ripple Vale. But the old embowered rectory is
still there, in which my father played and read, but mostly read,
for he was a studious child, in the years when Bonaparte, the
Corsican Ogre, was still a name to keep order in any nursery
near the sea. His father was not only Rector of Ripple, but for
the last ten years of his life had charge also of that grand old Norman church, then little more than a ruin, St Margaret-at-Cliffe,
which some returned Crusader, full of superstitious faith in the
virgin-martyr of Antioch, erected on the bleak South Foreland,
in order to purchase, as he imagined, an easy entrance into
heaven. Sumptuously restored since the days when my grandfather used to ride over with his pet spaniel trotting by his side
to hold an occasional service beneath its dilapidated roof, it now
serves the many holiday visitors to that break-neck nook, St
Margaret's Bay.

At the early age of nine my father was sent away to Merchant
Taylors' School in London, with the idea, perhaps, that he might
be safer there. It was too late. The infection which was already
draining the life out of his two small sisters had already laid its
grip on him, and he was soon hurriedly brought home again, to

---

[1] John French, 1st Earl of Ypres, was Commander-in-Chief of British
Forces in France, 1914-15. He died in 1925.

recover or to die. In effect he did neither. For though, after hovering for weeks between life and death, he began to get better, he was never again to enjoy that perfect health which Amiel, the Swiss philosopher, has aptly called the chief of liberties. The infection had fallen on what the doctors call the peritoneum, the covering of the bowel, for the Ripple cows must have been riddled with tubercle, and convalescence was, as usual, tedious and painful. We hear of him lying for hours on the hearthrug before the fire, with a soft cushion beneath his little inside to quiet his pain, and reading, reading, endlessly. His father had a well-stocked library, and he devoured book after book, histories, novels, restoration plays, some of which he confessed in after years had been better left unread, though to this omnivorous reading, continued throughout his early years, he no doubt owed not only his multifarious information, but much of the fluency, the charm, and the sense of style which are to be found both in his sermons and in everything else that came from his pen. Thus the long months of inaction were by no means wholly wasted, for his father's careful tuition, to which he had already owed so much, was resumed, and moreover, like every clever child, he was quite able to educate himself.

Eventually he recovered sufficiently to be sent away again to a London school, but this time to St Paul's, still housed in the shadow of the Cathedral, and here he remained from his twelfth to his nineteenth year. We hear nothing of games and playing-fields, but of long hours spent over Latin, Greek and even Hebrew. Left to themselves when out of school, the boys would play about anywhere, even, as I gather from one of my father's sermons, amongst the big stones with which the admired Waterloo Bridge was then being built. But there was no slacking in the class-room. In those days education was a most strenuous business. By the time a boy went up to the University he was expected to be able not only to translate fluently from two dead languages, but to compose in either, both prose and verse. To apply to my father a phrase which he once used of the Newman brothers, his intellect even before he left St Paul's had been 'refined and cultivated to the highest point by the most indefatigable study'. And his school rewarded it, on his leaving, with the greatest honour it was in its power to bestow, that of Pauline Exhibitioner.

Having gained an open scholarship at Worcester College, my father went up to Oxford at Michaelmas, 1821. In the following year his studies were again interrupted by a serious illness, probably a tubercular pneumonia, which nearly cost him his life, left on him permanent traces, and in the end no doubt led to his comparatively premature death. It was the day of drastic treatment, and the doctors did their best to slay him, but, having changed their tactics when the breath was nearly out of his body, were happily able to congratulate themselves on having saved his life. In spite of this set-back he succeeded in taking a First in Classics at the Michaelmas examination of 1824, being one of the four so placed.

His father, alas! was no longer alive to welcome the success to which he had himself so largely contributed. He had died quite unexpectedly of a stroke, in February 1823, before he had completed his sixty-fourth year, leaving behind him a bulky MS., *History of the Religious Wars in France*, on which he had been engaged for years, and which his widow, in despair of ever finding a publisher, eventually committed to the flames. Meanwhile, leaving the embowered rectory, which had witnessed so many tears, she had moved with her three surviving children to a house at Walmer, within a walk of her old home.

*

The present[1] Rector of Ripple, the Rev. Telford Varley, M.A.,

[1] i.e. in 1931.

himself a scholar and, like my grandfather, a Seatonian Prize-
man, brought to my knowledge, and has since taken the kindest
possible pains to decipher and transcribe a touching record of
my father's last days in his old home, in the form of some
Latin verses of his own composition, dated 1 April 1823
(exactly six weeks, that is, after his father's lamented death),
which, though written only in pencil inside an attic cupboard,
have been most marvellously preserved to the present day.
They not only give us a glimpse into the young undergraduate's
sorrowing, but as yet unawakened heart at a period of his life
– he was not yet twenty-one – of which he has left no other
record, but, for the few whom it may interest, they afford a
measure of his scholarship.

Till then, it must be remembered, he had led a cloistered life
amongst classical scholars and clerical dons, left over, as it
were, from the eighteenth century with its high sense of de-
corum and its horror of 'enthusiasm', to whom a sound knowledge of Latin and Greek and their literatures, with or without
the gift of apt quotation, was the one thing needful, the en-
viable hall-mark of a scholar and a gentleman. The dead hand
of the past, in fact, lay heavy on their shoulders, and nothing
short of a religious conversion, the still small voice heard in
their inmost souls, as my father heard it, could give them
strength to shake it off, and open their blind eyes to everlasting
issues. Years, indeed, after he had turned his back on a dry
classicism, and had learnt in suffering the courage of his emotions and the power of the living Word, I find my father in his
Diary dropping instinctively into Latin, when, worn out with
much preaching, he has to confess to some passing weariness of
mind or body. 'Ad omnia misere socors' – miserably indifferent
to everything – 'Otiose nihil faciendo inter nugas tempus con-
sumpsi' – too lazy to do any work I frittered away my time on
trifles. Such self-reproachful entries are not uncommon.

[28]

So, when the sudden death of his beloved father brought on him the first great shock and sorrow of his life, followed by the cruel wrench of having to turn out with his mother and family from Ripple's sheltered haven, the only home he had ever known, it was to his old school-friends, the Latin poets, and especially, I think, to Ovid, that he turned for the form and for the idiom in which to express his feelings and give his heart relief, little dreaming that his carefully pondered lines would ever come down to us. It had given him comfort, no doubt, to weave his misery into Latin verses, but that he should have inscribed them just where no one was likely to see them, and still less to understand them, might seem, to those who have no sense of providence, more like an act of blind instinct than one of deliberate purpose, the sort of inconsequent urge that prompts a dog to bury his bone. It was all his own secret, between himself and his 'dear heart', as the old Greeks have it, for now that his father was dead, there was no one in the house who could unravel what he had written; not his poor widowed mother, nor his elder sister, the 'My dear Fanny' of his letters, nor his half-witted elder brother, Augustus, nor pretty young Mary Ann, the baby of the family, with her hair still down her back.

The rectory of Ripple has been much enlarged since my father addressed to it his pitiful 'Vale, vale, in aeternum vale!' I like to think of him as pacing slowly up and down under the pink-budded apple trees of the rectory orchard, rehearsing his carefully studied lines while, ever and anon, half in sorrow for himself, his heart goes out to the dear form so newly laid in the earth beside his four dead children, underneath the ponderous paving stone still to be seen in the central aisle of Ripple church.

The garret, for I can call it nothing else, in which are the inscriptions, and which my father had shared since childhood with his elder brother, poor feckless 'Guck', is reached by a dark, break-neck stair, and is so low, when one gets there, that one can barely stand upright in it. The floor-space, twenty-one feet by twelve, gives room and little more for a narrow bed on either hand beneath the sloping rafters. It must have been in one of those two dark corners that my father lay for weeks as a boy, suffering agonies, as he tells us in one of his sermons,[1] from a barbarous treatment, the scars of which he carried to his grave. On account of a severe lung attack, it was thought necessary, among other drastic remedies, to keep open a perpetual blister on his chest, which produced a deep ulcerated wound with much 'proud flesh'. As the wound would not heal until this had been burnt away with caustic, his poor mother had to drag herself up the dark stairs every morning in order to touch this 'quick raw flesh', compared in the sermon to the leprosy of sin (Lev. 13:10), with bluestone (sulphate of copper). And 'Oh!' he adds, 'how I shrank from her hand!'

In the one and only upright wall, between the low door and the projecting fireplace and flues, there had once been an odd corner, which a previous rector had paid the village carpenter to board up and furnish with a light door, so that his young daughters might have no excuse for leaving their attic untidy. This *garde-robe*, this hanging cupboard, measures a little over two feet square, and fortunately its interior has never in all these hundred odd years been visited by painter's brush. It was on its virgin boards, on the planed 'reverse' of the door, and on the inside of the adjacent partition, that my father pencilled his verses on a level with his eyes. It was, indeed, the only spot on to which there fell sufficient light through the low and narrow casement. A garret! And yet, methought, as Mr Varley kindly threw the beam from his electric torch on to the faintly pencilled lines, how a long-past emotion, if deeply enough and genuinely felt, can light up even a garret!

[1] 'The Leper Diseased.' *Early Sermons*, Vol. III (1906), p. 237.

Such in essentials was the retired village rectory which my father and his housemates had to leave in exchange for a new, if less cramped, abode among strangers. 'Charae Aedes' he apostrophizes it, reverting with youthful pedantry to an obsolete spelling which still survives in our 'charity' and the French 'cher' –

(1) *Charae Aedes, quae me primis fovistis ab annis,*
    Qua primum lusi, tuta valete mea!
Ut te liquissem, me sors nimis improba cogit,
    Immemorem esse tui cogere nulla potest.

                    J. C. Philpot, April 1, 1823

To these not quite impeccable lines my kind friend of many years, the Poet-Laureate, has favoured me with the following translation:

> Dear rooms, in which from my first happy years,
> In childhood, I would play (safe, then), farewell!
> Though overwhelming Fate forces me from you,
> No Fate so strong can force me to forget you.

The second inscription, immediately below, consists of two lines which are not so clearly decipherable. The first is obviously a pentameter; the second, it may be inferred, was meant for a hexameter.

(2) *Nunquam te vita charior usque, pater,*
    Aspiciam positum . . te semper amabo.

                    J. C. P., Ap. 1, 1823

Translation, as before:

> Father, dearer than life, I shall never see you
> As one laid dead in the grave; I shall ever love you.

The above inscriptions are on the 'reverse' of the cupboard door. The next, which is in prose, is on the inside of the partition.

(3) *Haec in quibus a cunis usque ad
annum aetatis vigesimum felix habitavit
tuta linquere . . (invito?) scripsit.*

J. C. Philpot, Ap. 1, 1823

A word or two is here obscure. The sense is apparently:

O rooms! in which from the cradle until manhood
He who writes lived, both safe and happy, now
He leaves you, though unwilling.

Underneath this is written, quite plain to see:

(4) *Vale, vale, in aeternum vale!*

And still lower down a quotation from Virgil, which has not yet been identified.

Clearly enough, however, the classics helped to fashion his thinking.

*

Joseph Charles was now the only hope of the family, and he would soon be off his mother's hands. If he only took as good a degree as they all expected, he would be able to earn his living at Oxford as a private coach, until a Fellowship should fall vacant. Then would follow ordination, a public tutorship, followed in due course by a College living and further promotion. The ball would be at his feet. Given fair health and prudent conduct, there was scarcely any position within the Church of England to which he might not reasonably aspire. His dead father's dearest ambition might be realized. 'Why, but for the grace of God,' as one of his humble admirers once put it, 'he might have been a bishop', a bishop in lawn sleeves, like his old class-mates, Alfred Ollivant, of Llandaff, and James Prince Lee, the first Bishop of Manchester. But, as my father so often reminds us, God's thoughts are not our thoughts, nor His ways our ways.

[32]

All came off according to plan. He took his First in Greats, as already stated, and finding no difficulty in obtaining pupils as a private coach, he remained up at Oxford all through 1825 and well into 1826. He describes himself at this period as being not, indeed, what is called 'a gay young man', not living an immoral life, but still utterly dead in sin, 'without God and without hope in the world, looking forward to prospects in life, surrounded by worldly companions, and knowing as well as caring absolutely nothing spiritually for the things of God'.

Those years, indeed, of 1825–26, happened to be a most pregnant period in the history of the University. For in its quiet precincts the scene was even then being set and the actors prepared for a drama that was to convulse the religious world, in short, the Oxford Movement. It was in 1826, states my father in one of the last Reviews he ever wrote, that the leaven was first put into the meal. He was in the very centre of the original movement, he tells us, and personally knew some of its leading originators. Of these by far the most important in his eyes was the Rev. Charles Lloyd, D.D., Regius Professor of Divinity and eventually Bishop of Oxford, preferments which he owed largely to the esteem and gratitude of his former pupil, the rising statesman Robert Peel, who loved him as a brother, and took his counsel in all matters relating to the Church. The son of a most successful schoolmaster, Dr Lloyd when a youth had come under the influence of some of the cultured Catholic priests, whom the French Revolution had driven out of their homes. He had learnt much from them, and had formed a very different opinion of their piety and learning from that held by his orthodox brother-dons. Full of ambition to found a school of divinity at Oxford, which might be able to hold its own against its German rivals, the new Regius Professor started his historic private classes, comprising nearly all the rising men of the University, over whom, to quote my

B

father, 'from his ability, learning, strong mind, blended with a most amiable temper and disposition, he exercised a remarkable influence. With this private class Dr Lloyd read and discussed the history of the Council of Trent and that of the English Prayer Book, in such a way as to imbue his pupils with a respect for Roman Catholics and Roman Catholic doctrine, which to them was an entirely new notion.'[1] Some of these classes my father joined at the Bishop's special request, though, as he tells us, he did not much admire his teaching. He dreaded, no doubt, as well he might, its Romanizing tendency, for not a few of Charles Lloyd's pupils, including the most eminent of them, J. H. Newman, eventually seceded from the English Church. Bishop Lloyd lived long enough to ordain my father. In the following year, having delivered a powerful speech in the House of Lords in favour of Catholic Emancipation, for which he was snubbed at Court and lampooned in the Press, he died of a severe chill, with the abuse still ringing in his ears. His leading share in the Tractarian movement, which otherwise might have run a very different course, has been too often overlooked.

From his subsequent mention of them, I gather that among my father's intimate acquaintances at this date were four able and earnest-minded men, all of whom, for one reason or another, found themselves eventually compelled, like himself, to break away from the Church of England. They were John Henry Newman, the future Cardinal; Francis William, his younger brother; their fellow-lodger, the middle-aged Spanish ex-priest, Joseph Blanco White, who has left us one perfect sonnet and a most fascinating autobiography – 'a book', wrote Mr W. E. Gladstone in 1845, 'which rivets the attention and makes the heart bleed'; and, lastly, Frederick Oakeley, subse-

[1] *Reviews* (Reprinted from the *Gospel Standard*), Vol. II. (London, 1901), p. 619.

[34]

quently a Canon in the Roman Church and author of *Notes on the Tractarian Movement*, as well as of some entertaining reminiscences of Bishop Lloyd. John Keble at this date had already retired to a country parish, and my father never knew him personally, though he found much to criticize in *The Christian Year*. But I have heard him relate how once when returning as a young undergraduate to Oxford on the top of the coach, tired by his long journey out of Kent, he fell into a profound sleep, to find on awakening that a strong and sympathetic arm had been around him all the time, and had prevented his being pitched on to the road. That arm was John Keble's.

Of the Newmans, 'I once well knew two brothers', wrote my father not long before his death. 'I hardly like to mention their names, though none are better known through the breadth and length of the land. They were both men of most powerful intellect, refined and cultivated to the highest point by the most indefatigable study, and were distinguised ornaments of the famous University to which they belonged. Where and what are they now? One, the elder brother, whom I knew less intimately, is the most distinguished pervert from the Church of England that Rome has received; the other, once an intimate friend, an eminent professor of Classical learning, is now an avowed infidel.'[1] I will quote no more, especially as the last statement is hardly justified, since Francis Newman held and declared that none but a fool could be an atheist. Not less able, nor less ascetic than his elder brother, Francis Newman was of the same college as my father and became his intimate friend. Their ways for long ran strangely parallel, until they were separated by religious differences. For after resigning his Oxford Fellowship and seceding from the Established Church,

[1] *Gospel Standard*. Vol. XXXII, February 1866, p. 55. *Reviews*, Vol. II, p. 582.

Francis Newman became a private tutor in Ireland and was also baptized. Eventually, however, in his search, as he thought, for truth he threw off almost every tenet of the Christian faith, and my father could have no more to do with him. Some years ago a Syriac grammar was picked up on a second-hand bookstall, bearing their two autographs, 'J. C. Philpot to F. W. Newman', with the date 1829, doubtless a present on the eve of the younger man's hare-brained mission to Mesopotamia.

During the very years when my father used to preach every summer at the chapel in Gower Street, London, Francis Newman, as Professor of Latin, was holding his classes at University College, immediately opposite, though there is no record that they ever met. But I have been told that, before his own death in extreme old age, thirty years after my father's, F. W. Newman spoke very affectionately of his former friend.

4: The turning point

TOWARDS THE END OF 1825 A WEALTHY IRISH GENTLE-
man, posting home from London, broke his journey at Oxford
in the hope of finding and engaging there a resident tutor to
prepare his two sons for the University. Having failed in his
object, he was on the point of leaving early the next morning,
when some trivial accident happened to detain him. The delay
gave my father the chance of seeing him. He was offered the
post and accepted it, with such momentous consequences for
himself, that he ever afterwards attributed the whole incident
to nothing less than the direct intervention of Providence.

But I shall tell the story largely in his own words. I would
merely premise, for the sake of the general reader, that amongst
the earnest little communities to which he and William Tiptaft
eventually attached themselves, the demand was all for 'experimental', or, as I should prefer to call it, 'experiential' preaching. Authentic religious experience, to those who have known
it, is the most absorbing of topics, to those who have not, the
most wearisome and meaningless, like love-poems set before
a child. 'Were a Church-minister to talk about his experience
in the pulpit,' I find my father writing some years later, 'it
would rouse the drunken sexton from his nap, make the clerk's
hair stand upon his head, and terrify all the respectable part of
the congregation into the apprehension that the clergyman was
going out of his mind.' And yet what, for instance, could be
more experimental and therefore more consoling to a fellow-
sufferer and fellow-sinner, than parts of St Paul's *Epistles*, or
St Augustine's *Confessions*?

It is one thing, however, to confide one's soul-trouble to a sheet of paper in the privacy of one's study and quite another to avow it before a crowded chapel. That requires a picked minister, as well as a picked audience; on the one hand, a preacher of such deadly earnestness that he has the full courage of his emotions and the power to rise well above the baser levels of self-consciousness, and on the other, a simple, child-like people, who can understand and sympathize, and yet are quick to discern whether their minister's words ring false or true.

It is, by the way, the experimental, the 'felt' element in my father's sermons, which has kept them alive to this day, and carried them to every quarter of the globe where there happen to be what William James ('out of the depth of his ignorance', I can imagine my father objurgating) has dared to call 'sick souls'. And the discovery was all his own. 'I preached experience', he writes, 'before I knew there were such men as experimental preachers. I never stole a searching ministry from anyone. But I was searched and I searched others. When I was in the Church, I used to preach at times more searchingly than I have done since.' And, as we shall see, the lady of the manor invariably walked out when he assumed the black gown and climbed the pulpit stairs.

But to return to the Irish engagement: in a sermon, entitled 'Evidences Sealed and Open', delivered at Croydon in 1869, more than forty years after the event and just six months before his death, my father spoke thus:

'In the autumn of the year 1825 I was residing at Oxford, earning a comfortable livelihood by taking pupils, and looking forward to obtaining a still higher grade in my college. But quite unexpectedly, just at this time, a very eligible offer was made to me, and a high salary held out as an inducement, to go to Ireland for a short time for the purpose of educating for the University two sons of a gentleman of wealth and high position, whose country seat was not far from Dublin. Now, it was not to my interest to accept such an offer, as I was in good circumstances, and it was rather breaking my connection with my college, and so far somewhat interfering with my future prospects, to leave the University even for a short period; but no doubt the hand of God was in it, though I saw it not; for His thoughts were not my thoughts, nor His ways my ways. But I was tempted by the large salary, and went to Ireland in 1826, where I spent that year very happily and comfortably, for I had *everything that money could buy, or heart could wish*. But all this time I knew nothing experimentally of the things of God; for though highly moral, as far as regards man, and having a great respect for religion, the grace of God had not then touched my heart.

'But in the beginning of 1827, in the early spring, the Lord was pleased to bring upon me a very great trial and affliction, which I cannot name, but it was one of the greatest sorrows I ever passed through in my life, and it was in and under that affliction that the Lord was pleased, I have every reason to believe, to begin His work of grace upon my soul, and to do for me the things I have spoken of, in giving me the light of life, planting His fear in my heart, pouring out upon me the spirit of prayer, and communicating those other "sealed evidences" of the first kind, which I have laid before you; for though not without a hope in God's mercy, I was not favoured until some years after with any special manifestation of Christ.

'Now when I came back to Oxford in the autumn of 1827, the change in my character, life, and conduct was so marked that everyone took notice of it. I did not perceive myself, so distinctly, this outward change, though I well knew the inward; but it was very soon observed by others, and especially at my own college, and, in fact, very soon brought upon me a heavy

[39]

storm of persecution, which, with other concurring causes, eventually drove me from the University.

'I have no wish to put myself forward, and the only reason why I have mentioned these circumstances is to show, that wherever there is any real work of grace upon a man's heart, it will be made openly manifest; that others can see, as well as he can feel, that something has been wrought in his soul by a divine power, which has made him different from what he was before.

'It might perhaps have been easy for you, and cost you little sacrifice, to make a profession of religion, but it was not so with me. As Fellow of a college and looking forward to the honourable and advantageous office of public tutor, it was no small cross for me to break off old friendships and incur the dislike and contempt of the ruling authorities, and thus with my own hand pull down all my prospects of preferment and emolument for life. But there was a power resting on me in those days which made religion with me as everything, and the world as nothing.'

The 'gentleman of wealth and high position' with a country-seat near Dublin named Rathsallagh, who in the autumn of 1825 engaged young J. C. Philpot, then just turned twenty-three, to prepare his two sons for the University, was the Right Honourable Edward Pennefather, one of the most eminent lawyers of his time, and eventually Lord Chief Justice of the Court of King's Bench in Ireland. Descended from a family which claimed to have been settled there before the Normans came, he was himself the father of ten children, the eldest of whom was a tall, beautiful, serious-minded girl of marriageable age, named Anne. The sons who were to be my father's pupils were Edward, aged seventeen, and William, a year or so his junior, who afterwards took orders. There were two younger brothers, and a nurseryful of sisters, one of whom eventually married a Bishop of Ossory, while another became Countess of Courtown.

In this luxurious home, not far though it was from the peasants' miserable, smoky cabins which so horrified him, my father had a private study, a horse to ride, appreciative pupils, and ample leisure, some of which he was able to devote to the poor ragged children in the Sunday-school. And for fifteen months all went well. Then in the early spring of 1827 there happened that which was surely ordained to happen. The good-looking young tutor fell desperately in love with the daughter of the house, fair Anne, and she, one gathers, quite deeply enough with him. In their young comely innocence they seemed made for each other, though the youth, it is true, had a delicate chest, and next to no money. But it was not to be, and after an all too brief dream of bliss they had to part for ever, after exchanging pathetic little keepsakes, including a pocket Cowper, the three choicely bound volumes of which are still among my dearest treasures. The great love-stories of the world have seldom, if ever, been happy ones, for happiness, it has been said, has no history. But here, as we know, it was more than individual and earthly happiness which was at stake. Had the boy-and-girl marriage been allowed, Oxford might have boasted of one more erudite classical scholar, and the Church of England of one more be-gaitered dignitary, but thousands of humble Christians would have lost the wise counsel of a fellow-pilgrim, and the *Gospel Standard* through thirty-five years a staunch and able defender of the truth as it is in Jesus.

The parents acted firmly, kindly, and wisely, as indeed they were *meant* to act. A delicate youth, whose only fixed income – as Fellow of a college – depended on his remaining single, was obviously no suitable mate for a high-born damsel reared

[41]

in luxury. The girl was sent away to weep out her heart among friends, while the young tutor stayed on to complete his engagement amid everything, oh irony! 'that money could buy or heart could wish'.

He made no secret in after years of the intensity of his love or the depth of his despair. 'I have often wetted the pommel of my saddle with tears,' he tells a friend, 'amid the lonely valleys of the Wicklow hills, or galloped half-distracted along the sea-shore where no eye could see, or ear could hear me cry and groan, sometimes from natural trouble and sometimes in pouring out my soul before the Lord.' He never married while the lady lived, and cherished her memory as devoutly as Dante that of his Beatrice. At the end of his engagement his pupils had presented him with a handsome brass-bound desk. On his return to Oxford he brought it back with him, and in its most secret drawer a few poor withered flowers, his loved one's parting gift. Wellnigh forty years later, when my elder sister came upon them as she was tidying the desk, she was sharply bidden to leave them untouched. They were still there when he died.

To Anne Pennefather,[1] it might almost be said, my father owed his own salvation. In losing her, had he not, after long pain and grief, eventually found Christ? It was as if she had been sent into his life expressly to show him the way, the thorny way to Calvary. So on my mother's lips, though never on his, the name of Anne Pennefather became one to be remembered and mentioned with tender awe, though on no account to be breathed outside the house.

[1] The much loved servant of the Lord, Rev. William Pennefather (1816–73), of whom it was said that to describe his life in detail would be 'like trying to catch sunbeams', was Anne's first cousin. He held various benefices in the Church of England and ended as Vicar of St Jude's, Mildmay Park, Islington. His *Life and Letters* ran through four editions.

It was a little over four years after her bereavement, if such one may venture to call it, that Anne Pennefather finally consented to bestow her hand and what was left of her heart on Mr Wade Browne, a wealthy Cambridge graduate, some ten years her senior, who had been a great traveller and could give her a stately home on the borders of Wiltshire. But Anne, it is grievous to relate, was granted little more than six years of married life in these ideal surroundings, most of them spent in childbearing. She brought into the world first two daughters and then two sons, after which, like Rachel, she was taken, leaving her children motherless. In my father's diary[1] for 1837, the only one he had not the heart to destroy, are these two pitiful entries:

'Sept. 6. A. P. *infantem peperit*' (bore a child).
'Sept 29. A. P. *mortua est*' (is dead).

On her tombstone in Monkton-Farleigh church, her sorrowing husband paid this touching tribute to her memory:

'She was talented, gentle, compassionate and self-denying, and a most affectionate wife and mother, and from her childhood a willing and devoted servant of God, altogether relying on the merits and intercession of her Saviour.

'A woman that feareth the Lord shall be praised; she shall rejoice in time to come.'

*

No lapse of years could efface the months of blessed anguish spent in Ireland from my father's memory. They obtrude even

[1] From the same diary we learn that the texts which he chose for his two sermons on the Sunday after he had heard of her death were, 'The righteous shall hold on his way', and 'He discovereth deep things out of darkness, and bringeth out to light the shadow of death' (Job 12:22).

in his most serious Reviews: 'I resided in Ireland for eighteen months at one period of my life,' he tells his readers, 'a time never to be forgotten by me whilst life endures, though more than twenty-seven years have rolled away since that warm summer eve, fresh to my memory as yesterday, when I left its green shores, and the beautiful Wicklow mountains faded on my sight. I have taught in the Sunday-school a class of bare-footed, ragged little fellows, whose habiliments smelling of turf, the least unpleasant of their odours, were sufficiently repulsive to the young collegian fresh from the elegancies of Oxford; and remember, almost with a smile, to this day the careful way in which I had to put down my foot, lest it should inadvertently tread on some of the many naked surrounding toes. I have seen and talked with the poor peasants in their smoky, miserable cabins, and been almost horrified by the spectacle of Irish misery. And I may add, that I have every reason to love Ireland, for there, in the early spring of 1827, the first beams of light and life visited my previously dead and benighted soul, and Irish valleys and mountains witnessed the first tears and prayers that went up out of the heart to the throne of grace.'[1]

The revolution in his own spirit was so intense, so complete, so unexpected, and on the face of it so inconsequent, that he could never afterwards attribute it to anything short of a divine intervention, an unmistakable 'call'. Indeed, in after years, and it sometimes got him into difficulty, he was inclined to question, or at least to submit to a very jealous scrutiny, any conversion which had been less marked or less sudden than his own, although at the same time he was as suspicious of false fire and 'enthusiasm' as any Oxford don. Almost from that

---

[1] *Gospel Standard*. February 1855, p. 60. Reprinted in *Reviews*, Vol. I, p. 379. The first person singular has been substituted for the editorial 'We'.

moment he became a humble follower and lover of our Lord, and governed all his life by the truth which he believed had in that moment of vision been 'impressed upon his conscience very powerfully and very distinctly by the finger of God', the truth, namely, that there is no authentic religion which is not the immediate particular gift and grace of the Holy Spirit, 'that one can know nothing but by divine teaching, have nothing but by divine giving, be nothing but by divine making'.

'All true religion,' he writes a few years later, in words which give no doubt a faithful picture of that emotional convulsion, remembered in tranquillity – 'all true religion has a beginning, and a beginning, too, marked, clear and distinct. That the entrance of divine light into the soul, the first communications of supernatural life, the first manifestations of an unknown God, the first intercourse of man with his Maker – that all these hitherto unfelt, unthought of, uncared for, undesired transactions should take place in the soul and the soul be ignorant of them, should know neither their time nor their place, is a contradiction. The evidence of *feeling* is as strong, as distinct, as perceptible as the evidence of *sense*. . . . A man's body is alive to every feeling from a pin scratch to a mortal wound. The heart cannot flutter, or omit for a single second its wonted stroke, without a peculiar sensation that accompanies it, notices it, and registers it. Shall feelings then be the mark and evidence of natural life, and not of spiritual? Thus *feeling* is the first evidence of supernatural life – a feeling compounded of two distinct sensations, one referring to God, and the other referring to self. The same ray of light has manifested two opposite things . . . God and self, justice and guilt, a holy law and a broken commandment, eternity and time, the purity of the Creator and the filthiness of the creature. And these he sees as personal realities involving all his happiness, or all his misery in time and in eternity.

'Thus it is with him as though a new existence had been communicated, as if for the first time he had found there was a God. It is as though all his days he had been asleep and were now awakened—asleep upon the top of a mast, with the raging waves beneath; as if all his past life were a dream, and the dream were now at an end. He has been hunting butterflies, blowing soap-bubbles, angling for minnows, picking daisies, and idling life away like an idiot or a madman. . . . A sudden peculiar conviction has rushed into his soul. One absorbing feeling has seized fast hold of it, and well-nigh banished every other. "There is a God and I am a sinner before Him. What shall I do? Where shall I go? What will become of me? Mercy, O God! Mercy, mercy! I am lost, ruined, undone! Fool, madman, wretch, monster that I have been! I have ruined my soul. O my sins, my sins! O eternity, eternity!" '[1]

One more experimental passage from the same sermon is worth quoting. He is speaking of the hour when hope begins to conquer despair, and infinite compassion to appear in the place of infinite justice. 'The budding forth of hope and the opening of this heavenly flower is a season never to be forgotten. Well do I remember the place—a little garden, hidden by buildings and overgrown with shrubs, where this flower opened in my soul. But the buildings could not hide it, nor the evergreens shade it, nor the damp close it. The bud opened, the flower burst forth, and at the same moment the eye looked up, and the mouth uttered, "Whom have I in heaven but Thee? and there is none upon earth that I desire beside Thee".'

[1] *Winter afore Harvest, or The Soul's Growth in Grace.* 1837, p. 18.

5: Return to Oxford

IT CAN BE EASILY IMAGINED THAT WITH SUCH A TEM-
per and with such a creed, my father's position when he came
back to Oxford to take up his Fellowship in the autumn of
1827 proved a desperately thorny one. Deeply as one must
sympathize with the passionate young visionary, torn with
suffering, and contending for the truths which he thought had
been supernaturally revealed to him, one cannot help feeling
just a trifle sorry for his amiable, well-meaning, self-satisfied
superiors, level-headed men of business, intent upon sustaining
the tranquil order of the world and the University, and on
training up a constant succession of young hopefuls into due
respect for the Church, the Throne, the British Constitution,
and two, if not three, dead languages. Here was their prize
pupil, as good a classical scholar as they had turned out for
years, whom they had meant to be a help and an honour and
an asset to their college, returned upon their hands an unprofitable changeling, a piece of grit between their smoothly rolling
wheels, an intemperate will, not to be harnessed to their very
excellent and far from unprofitable purpose.

Meanwhile he was no better satisfied than they. 'Oft-
times,' he tells us, 'seated after dinner in the Common room
with the other Fellows, amidst all the drinking of wine and the
hum and buzz of conversation in which I took no part, I have
been secretly lifting up my heart to the Lord.' To quote him
again: 'I stand before Him whose eyes are as flames of fire, to
search out the secrets of my heart. And what is this poor, vain
world with all its gilded clay, painted-touch-wood honours and
respectability, and soap-bubble charms? What is all the wealth

[47]

of the Church piled up in one heap, compared to a smile of a loving Saviour's countenance?' What could the Oxford of 1827 make of a man who took his religion so seriously, so tactlessly as all that – an Oxford, by the way, which was divided between orthodox high-church scholars, as fond of old port as of ancient lore, and the earnest young *dilettanti* of Oriel Common room, jocularly known as 'the men of the tea-pot'? Surely his proper place, if one may apply the double metaphor without offence, was not among the eminently respectable scribes and pharisees with their mundane values, but with publicans and sinners, with the despised and rejected of men. And sooner or later he would find it out.

Some of the Fellows, one is glad to learn, were kind and considerate to the tormented youth, but their head, the Provost, who seems to have taken a violent dislike to him, soon found occasion to inform him that he would be permanently excluded, on account of his religious views, from any and every college office. As the views in question included nothing whatever contrary to the Articles of the Established Church, which the Provost had himself subscribed, my father was quite justified in resenting the decision as arbitrary and despotic. There was, however, no appeal, and the career of public tutor, to which he had so long looked forward and for which he was so eminently qualified, being thus definitively closed to him, the only alternative was parish work.

He had no great difficulty in finding a curacy near enough to Oxford to allow of his still retaining the pleasant Fellow's rooms which had been allotted to him, overlooking the beautiful Worcester College gardens, and he was accordingly ordained by Bishop Lloyd, in 'the Cathedral Church of Christ in Oxford' on Trinity Sunday, 1 June 1828, side by side, as already mentioned, with that gifted youth, E. B. Pusey, who in his middle years, though for very different reasons, was destined to encounter even wider abuse and opprobrium than my father.

Thus rudely shaken out of conceit with the University and all the stately scholarship it represented, henceforth, like another Tertullian, he deliberately turned away from classical literature—'a mere phosphorus light, composed of dead men's brains, too faint to illuminate, too cold to kindle'—in order to bathe his spirit in the uncompromising sincerity of the Holy Scriptures, finding more food for his heart in a single chapter of Isaiah than in the noblest chorus of Aeschylus, more saving truth in the first few verses of the Epistle to the Ephesians than in all the Dialogues of Plato. He ceased, in short, from studying the word of man, in order that he might the more diligently search the Word of the living God. For whoever believes as confidently as he did that the Scriptures are divinely and liter-ally inspired, will search them, as you search a living face, for an answer to a definite appeal, such as no dead portrait can possibly give. Commentaries he held to be useless, except for occasional textual help. They usually failed one where most required. The light to be trusted was bestowed from above. 'As the blessed Spirit of all truth is pleased to shine upon a text,' I find my father writing a few years later, 'a peculiar light is thrown upon it, a peculiar beauty, force, truth and power seem to shoot forth from every part of it, so that every word appears dipped in heavenly dew, and every expression to drip with honey. Whenever a text has been thus opened to me, I have seen a fulness and tasted a sweetness, which carried with it its own evidence that they (*sic*) were the words of the living God.'[1]

Luther in 1521 expressed a similar view in his Preface to the Magnificat, 'No one can understand God, or God's Word,

---

[1] *The Heir of Heaven*, etc. (London, 1837), p. 8. (New Edition, 1926), p. 2.

unless it is revealed to him by the Holy Spirit; but no one can receive anything of the Holy Spirit, unless he himself experience it. In experience the Holy Spirit teaches as in His own school, and outside that nothing of value can be learned.'

Nevertheless, though his well-thumbed classics were relegated to the shelf, for they were not sent to the hammer until seven years later, he set himself to study with all the greater diligence the languages in which the sacred writings have come down to us, and in this he persevered throughout the rest of his life. Seldom a day passed on which he did not devote a full hour every morning to the Hebrew Testament, and a like period every evening to the Greek. I can well recall how sometimes his voice would be heard booming through our little house at Stamford, as he attempted, however imperfectly, to recapture the very native accents of some Messenger of God, whose bones had crumbled to dust long centuries ago.

*

Seven miles south of Oxford, divided from each other by the little river Thame, are two insignificant villages, which are known to the cartographer as Stadhampton and Chiselhampton, but to their rustic inhabitants as Stadham and Chiselton. The latter, as its name indicates, lies salubriously upon the gravel and contains the seat of the Squire. But Stadham, with the church, is on the gault, a vicious subsoil, and has been described by my father as 'an unhealthy village with a damp green and miry roads'. The rector being long past work, my father became his perpetual curate, an obsolete form of incumbency which meant all the work and little pay. It was an unfortunate choice for a delicate man. So long as he was able to sleep and board luxuriously in Oxford, he did not suffer, but the plan of working his parish from his Fellow's rooms barely survived a winter's trial. The fatigue of the daily ride in all weathers on the top of his parish work proved too arduous for him. 'A great gulf seemed placed also in my feelings between my former friends and myself, and one day in particular, as I was sitting on my horse near the college gates, it was so impressed on my mind that Oxford was no place for me that I gladly turned my back on it and went to reside permanently at Stadhampton.' 'Moreover, my mind being at that time much impressed by, and taken up with, divine realities, I desired to live a separate, godly life, and devote myself to the care of my parish and the good of the souls of men.'

He took rooms at a farmhouse on the green, close to Stadhampton church and thither he had removed himself and his once beloved books shortly before the critical meeting with William Tiptaft aforementioned. It was a rough, ill-fed, ill-tended life after the ordered comfort of Oxford, and the record of the seven lonely years he passed there is one of constant ill-health, over-strain and mental misery. It was partly his own fault, for he had not yet learnt to spare himself. His services on Sunday, to say nothing of his weekday work, would have tried even a robust frame. He began the day by teaching in the Sunday school, then walked with the children to church, where he conducted the service alone, and preached *extempore* for seldom less than an hour. At the afternoon service he preached for another hour and then had the children up to the schoolhouse, poor mites! to hear how much of the sermons they had remembered and how much understood. In the evening, in his own room, he expounded a few verses of Scripture to anyone who cared to come, closing the day with prayer.

Almost from the first he had antagonized the Squire and his wife, partly by declining to lunch with them on the Lord's Day, as his predecessors had invariably done, and partly, I think, by his honest outspokenness in the pulpit. And they were almost the only people of his own standing in the neighbour-

[51]

hood. 'I was raw indeed when I went there,' he admitted later on, 'but had many trials, and few friends or counsellors in them. I often acted very rashly and hastily, and frequently mistook my own spirit for the Spirit of the Lord'–a not uncommon delusion, one may add, which has caused more persecution in the world than almost anything else.

Meanwhile his church began to fill and soon, though large for its purpose, to become uncomfortably crowded. From all the neighbourhood people flocked to hear him. On one occasion, we are told, hearers from as many as eighteen different parishes were identified among his congregation. He had, indeed, a lofty ideal of what a sermon should be. 'A ministry of this kind,' he writes, 'gushing out of the preacher's heart and mouth as a spring of living water, is as different from a hard, dead, cut-and-dry ministry, based on study and premeditation and commentaries, as a living breathing man from a withered skeleton. Cold, dry learning is not wanted in the pulpit. What is wanted there is experience in the heart, life and feeling in the soul, and such a measure of divine power resting on the spirit as shall clothe the ideas that spring up with clear, simple, suitable language within the comprehension of the most uneducated hearer. A ministry of this kind will be fresh, original, stamped with a peculiar impress, and will carry with it a weight and power which manifest its divine Author.'[1] This was written, it must be admitted, many years after he had left the Church of England, but the lesson had been learnt at Stadhampton.

Even today, when the pulpit has to compete with the Sunday Press, the 'wireless', and the 'pictures', any really earnest preacher can fill his church or chapel. But a hundred years ago reading was a rare accomplishment in country villages, and the pulpit provided the only means whereby a poor farm-

[1] *Gospel Standard*. March 1852, Vol. XVIII, p. 97.

labourer could be helped for a moment to forget his daily cares, and be taken out of himself into a wider air. Many, no doubt, came to listen to my father out of curiosity, and perhaps to hear each other soundly trounced, but there was a remnant of picked souls who found more in his message than mere entertainment, and these became his friends and faithful followers even long after he had left them, *cittadini d'una vera città* (citizens of the true city). To these he had opened a door out of their ignorance and poverty, to these he had given, in Santayana's phrase, 'a new world to live in', and, in Nietzsche's, such a 'transvaluation of values' that they never again need envy the rich their wealth, the scholar his interest, or the artist his emotion. Had they not discovered the Bible? Had they not been brought face to face with Christ? There are always, by the way, poor hungry souls who think they know the sort of religion they want better than a whole bench of bishops, and they will walk miles upon miles to get it.

But now another figure appears upon the scene. A second stream has to be traced to its source, and for a time we must leave my father and his troubles.

6: William Tiptaft

THE YOUNGEST OF FIVE SURVIVING CHILDREN, THREE
boys and two girls, William Tiptaft was born on 16 February
1803 (almost exactly a hundred years after John Wesley) at
Braunston, a sequestered village in the valley of the Gwash,
close to the borders of Leicestershire, but within an hour's
walk of Oakham, the county-town of Rutland. Here, on the
evidence of the Parish Registers, his family had been settled
certainly since the accession of Queen Elizabeth, if not much
earlier, and they belonged to that sterling class of smaller
gentry, farming their own land, which once formed the back-
bone of England, and which in its day produced so many distinguished men.

For at least seven generations, William Tiptaft's ancestors
had tilled and grazed their freehold acres, and latterly each in
his turn had served his year as High Sheriff of his diminutive
county, the last to hold that office being William's eldest
brother, James, in 1819. They intermarried with their neighbours, the Cheseldens and the Burnabys. If the Napoleonic
wars spelt prosperity to the yeoman class, the slump in prices
that followed the peace went far to ruin them. Some sold the
land they had held for generations and joined the ranks of
tenant-farmers, others more wisely went with their families to
the Colonies and carried their habits of industry and sobriety
with them. Before William Tiptaft came of age most of the
ancestral property had been sold or divided, and much of his
portion, as we shall see, eventually found its way into the
pockets of the poor. Braunston church is still partly paved
with Tiptaft gravestones, but the village, sequestered amongst
its fertile pastures, knows them no more.

In his *Memoir of William Tiptaft*, my father traces many of his friend's characteristic qualities to his mother, and notably 'that kindness and liberality to the poor, that amiability of disposition, and that high sense of duty and religion, which, though afterwards heightened and set off by grace, would in any case have been marked features in his natural character'.

The little river Gwash – Drayton's 'wandering Wash' – which, descending from the Leicestershire hills, falls into the Welland just below Stamford, divides the tiny county of Rutland into two almost equal parts. Some seven or eight miles below the point where it passes through Braunston, and half-way between Stamford and Oakham, there lies on the skirts of the Gwash valley a pleasant village, Edith Weston, which for close on a thousand years has preserved the memory of the fair Editha, the widow of Edward the Confessor, and its proprietress until her death in 1075. Here in the eighteenth century, and for how much earlier I know not, there lived and flourished another gentle yeoman family, the Tomblins, who also supplied sheriffs to their county, and tombstones to their churchyard. Sarah Tomblin married William Keal of Oakham, surgeon, and there are tablets to their memory in Oakham church; while Elizabeth, her younger sister, with whom we are chiefly concerned, married James Tiptaft of Braunston. Of him not much is known, except that he was of sufficient repute to be appointed Sheriff of Rutland in 1792, four years before his wife's brother, Robert Tomblin, was picked for that responsible office.

Having lost his father when he was a child of eight, and his mother six years later, while he was still a schoolboy at Uppingham, young William had thenceforth made his home and spent his holidays with his sister Deborah, twelve years his senior, in the roomy old house at the top of Oakham market-place, around which much of our later narrative will centre. On 11 June 1816, thirteen years to the very day, as he tells us, before he first met my father at Wallingford, Deborah Ward Tiptaft had married her first cousin, William Tomblin Keal, who had just come back with a St Andrews' M.D. to take over from his father, also William Keal, his medical practice, as well as the old house, which he had enlarged to accommodate his own growing family. And Mr and Mrs Keal – for in those days a mere surgeon did not flaunt his title of Doctor, even if he had one – were my maternal grandparents.

After nine years at Uppingham School, which before Dr Thring was neither much better nor much worse than its local rivals, William Tiptaft, being intended for the Church, went up to St John's College, Cambridge, as a 'pensioner' in October 1821. 'He was not', writes my father, 'what is called a reading-man, but being full of good temper and high spirits and very fond of conversation, his rooms were much the resort of men like himself, not studious and yet not altogether idle, moral, not gay and dissipated, yet cheerful and of that Athenian spirit, which is ever enquiring "Is there anything new?"'

Though when I first knew him, his fine, silky hair had turned to silver, he must have been a very good-looking youth with his delicate aquiline features. While still an undergraduate he came home to Oakham one vacation in the early stage of what was, no doubt, a severe attack of typhoid fever, in those days a very prevalent and terribly fatal malady. For weeks he lay between life and death. It brought him, as can be easily imagined, into peculiarly intimate relations with his brother-in-law, Mr Keal, who in those nurseless days tended him night and day with such watchful and devoted skill that he eventually recovered, while two of his fellow-students who had taken the infection at the same time fell victims to it. 'But when God has a work for a man to do,' to quote my father, 'he is immortal till that work is done.' William Tiptaft, we may be sure, gave thanks where thanks were due. Nevertheless, to save the soul of the man, who under providence had saved his body from an untimely and unregenerate grave, became for him, as soon as he realized the danger of his own, a matter of passionate concern, the driving force behind many long and earnest letters.

Fully recovered from this illness, he went up for his public examination with the other students of his year in January 1825, and secured a creditable place in what is called the 'Poll'. He had a remarkable natural talent for arithmetic, 'and I have heard him say', writes my father, 'that he answered all the arithmetical questions almost as fast as they were brought to him by the examiners'.[1] 'In after life, however, he did not display any great acquaintance with academic lore.' In the following summer, that he might be able to satisfy some episcopal examining chaplain, though which he as yet knew not, he went to study divinity under a private tutor at Charlton Kings, near Cheltenham, and while there formed an acquaintance, which was pregnant for him with important issues. He contracted, in fact, an intimate friendship with Edward Coleridge, of an old Somersetshire family, who soon after became an Eton master, and a son-in-law of Dr Keate, the famous castigator, but also, as it happened, a Canon of Windsor.

It was through this acquaintance that William Tiptaft was selected as his curate at Treborough, Somerset, by Archdeacon Trevelyan, whose brother, Sir John, had a beautiful seat and large estates in the neighbourhood. Having satisfied the exam-

---

[1] Thanks to his wonderful memory he was, I have been told, in his younger days a very fine whist player, and when he and his handsome cousin, my great-aunt, Rebecca Keal, were partners, they were almost sure to win. She was eventually converted through him and remained until the end of a long life a very consistent and much respected Christian.

ining chaplain as to his 'virtuous and pious life' and also as to his 'learning and knowledge in the Holy Scriptures' (I quote from the usual certificate), he was ordained by the Bishop of Bath and Wells at the beautiful cathedral of Wells in March 1826. Treborough is only a small village of some 130 souls, and here William Tiptaft remained until the beginning of 1828, and here, according to his own account, his soul was quickened in January 1827. Meanwhile he had so thoroughly satisfied his superior that he was thought to have earned a more responsible position. In January 1828, accordingly, Archdeacon Trevelyan passed him on to his own son, the vicar of the adjacent but much larger parish of Stogumber, with a population of nearly a thousand. Here too, as in Treborough, he seems to have won golden opinions on account of his zeal, his earnestness, and his devotion to the cause of the poor.

'I have always thought', writes my father, 'that his distinguishing feature, through the whole of his spiritual life, was the fear of God, manifesting itself in a most self-denying, upright, practical walk and conduct. Others might have greater natural abilities and more shining pulpit gifts; but where shall we find one, either minister or private Christian, who, from the beginning to the end of his profession, lived and walked like him? Truly in him "the fear of the Lord was a fountain of life to depart from the snares of death".' This fear, as the beginning of wisdom, was implanted in his soul when he was at Treborough, and, if at first not very deep, was genuine. Its first effect was to separate him from the world, to lead him to solitude and reflection, and give him an earnestness and seriousness of character which were in striking contrast with the lightness and frivolity of his college life. Its second effect was to set him to work; and, as he had now a large parish, it gave him an ampler field. Feeling his hands on the stilts of the plough, looking on the congregation as specially entrusted to

[58]

him to plough it and make it bear a crop for God, and animated by a fresh and new stimulus, he drove it strongly and firmly through the thick clods.

'As regards his own experience at this time, I never heard him speak much of it beyond these two things: 1, The separation of spirit which he felt from the world; and 2, the earnestness with which he read religious books, and especially any prayers which he could procure. The reason, I think, of this latter point was that he found in them his feelings and desires put into words, and thus felt an echo to them in his own bosom.'

Meanwhile he had become on very friendly and intimate terms with Edward Coleridge and his newly-married wife, during their visits into Somersetshire, and one day in mid-winter, 1829, he unexpectedly received the following letter:

'Eton College, 22 January 1829

'My dear Tiptaft: I find, on my arrival here from Dr Keate's, that the living of Sutton Courtney, near Abingdon, is to be given away in about ten days or so by the Canons of Windsor. They are anxious to give it to a good man; and if you like the account herein contained of it, I think I could insure it you. Three thousand souls to take care of; a good, but not a very large house, value from £120 to £150 per annum. If you think it worth your notice, write immediately a letter, with what testimonials you can collect, to the Hon. and very Rev. the Dean and Canons of Windsor, soliciting it, and I will take care that it is backed up.

In great haste, yours very heartily,
EDWARD COLERIDGE'

As he had for some time been anxious to exchange his curacy for a position of greater authority and independence, he at once bestirred himself to obtain the requisite testimonials.

[59]

'As deans and chapters', to quote from the *Memoir*, have always plenty of eager applicants for any vacant place of preferment which they may have to give away, and amongst them sons-in-law, nephews, cousins, and a whole tribe of poor relations in the curate line, almost without end, it seems a singular, and, indeed, a marked incident in providence, that they should have in this case departed from their usual course, and entertained some care for the parish instead of thinking only of their hungry candidates. They wanted a man, if not with a soul above lucre, yet with a pocket above it – one who would do the parish some good, instead of the parish doing it all to him. All honour to the dean and canons for this considerable thoughtfulness. They little foresaw, however, on whom they were about to confer their living, and what secret designs of providence were wrapped up in their anxiety to give it to a good man – good according to their sense of the word, which so far was honest and sincere. Our friend, however, at once set himself to procure the requisite testimonials to character and qualifications; and as these were of a superior kind, and were signed by such influential persons as Archdeacon Trevelyan, and, I believe, Archdeacon Law, they would necessarily carry with them much weight and authority. Considerable delay, however, had taken place, and so late were they in being sent that but for a singular and providential circumstance the living would have been disposed of before they arrived.' This is graphically told in the following letter from Mrs Coleridge:

Eton, Tuesday 3 *February* 1829

'My dear Sir: By this same post you will probably receive a letter from the chapter-clerk of Windsor, informing you that you are vicar of Sutton Courtney, as which we hail you most cordially, and sincerely hope that we shall not have been the means of removing you from your present abode of peace and happiness to one of trouble and annoyance. There are very few persons whom we should ever have thought of proposing for such an arduous and unprofitable piece of preferment; but we know your peculiar turn for parochial duties, that you wished for something to call your own, and had the good fortune of being so situated with regard to pecuniary affairs as not to make the value of the living a great object.

'The dean and chapter of Windsor were glad to hear of you, as all the candidates they have had have been a few distressed men, who only wished for the living for the sake of the emolument (little as it is), and would never have had the means of doing good in the parish, if even they had the inclination. My husband is so entirely occupied with his own duties today that it would have been quite impossible for him to write before post-time; he, therefore, hopes you will accept his congratulations through me, and believe that his own silence is quite unavoidable. You owe your getting the living merely to a lucky chance, for the chapter met at twelve o'clock this morning to give away the living, and no testimonials had then arrived from you, so that we knew not whether you had changed your mind about the thing or not. (Why were you not wise enough to write by the post to say you had sent them?) When twelve o'clock came and nothing had arrived, we gave the thing up in despair, and my father went up to Windsor quite disappointed; but at half-past one your packet appeared, and though we knew it was then almost hopeless, we sent a man up to Windsor with it, post-haste, and most fortunately it arrived when they were just in the midst of their debate, which would have been over long before had they not, by the greatest good luck in the world, been detained an hour in rectifying some mistake in a lease, which they had first to sign.

'My father desires me to tell you that you must be instituted and inducted before the 26th of this month, but that you are not required to come here unless you like it, as they will send you the presentation, and all your business is with the bishop.

'You must write immediately to say what is your university rank, as they know not whether to enter you in the presentation as M.A. or B.A.

'If you should deem it proper to come on to Windsor, we shall be delighted to see you. In the meantime, believe me to remain,

Ever yours sincerely,
MARY COLERIDGE'

'On what minute points', again to quote my father, 'do the most important matters sometimes hang! But for the delay caused by the examination of lease, Tiptaft would not have been vicar of Sutton Courtney, or been brought into that neighbourhood where his labours were to be so abundantly blessed. Humanly speaking, I myself should never have known him, never enjoyed the benefit of his friendship, counsel, or example; and, as much of my life for many years has been connected with my intimacy with him, an important link would have been wanting in my own chain of Providence.'

Before he left Stogumber he preached a farewell sermon, from 1 Sam. 12:23, 24, which he afterwards published, at the request of his parishioners. As far as I can remember, for it is some years since I read it, there is nothing particular in it beyond a general tone of sincerity and earnestness. I have no doubt that he was exceedingly popular at Stogumber, and his leaving it was much regretted, especially by the poor. All who knew him will, I believe, agree with me that one of the most marked features of his character was the sympathy he felt with the poor, and the thoroughness with which he identified himself with their feelings, views and interests. In this point I never saw in his rank of life, I will not say his equal, but any one who in the least approached him. He was eminently the poor man's friend, not in a condescending, patronizing way, as if he were out of mere kindness lowering himself, or doing them an honour by friendly intercourse, but as one with them, if not in station, yet in sympathy and feeling. And I must do his poorer friends the credit of bearing my testimony that I never, or, at least, very rarely, knew any who took advantage of his kindness to treat him with disrespect or undue familiarity. Though free, he was never familiar; and thus each party preserved his place, avoiding, by mutual respect, those liberties which so often break up close intimacy.'

William Tiptaft was 'instituted and inducted' to his new living in February 1829, and soon took up his quarters at the vicarage, a pleasant, comfortable house which, since it was, for all he knew, to be his permanent abode, 'he furnished very suitably and nicely'.

7: The Vicar of Sutton Courtney

BEFORE DIDCOT JUNCTION HAD PLANTED ITSELF IN the vicinity, Sutton Courtney might be described as sunk in the depths of the country. It had, however, a quiet life of its own. Abingdon, its market town, was only three miles distant, a paper-mill gave employment to many hands, and in those days of barge-traffic it was a fairly busy distributing centre. It consisted, and still consists, of one wide straggling street bearing away south from the river, with vicarage and church a little way down on the left and, at the end, embowered in trees, the ancient manor house, once an appanage of the big monastery at Abingdon. All around lies the fruitful vale of Berks with its many scattered villages.

Such was Sutton Courtney when William Tiptaft first went to live there in the spring of 1829. Now it lies with crumbling wharves and derelict mill, above the loveliest of backwaters, but quite away from the navigable stream, so that the tripper, as he hurries, or is hurried through Culham Cut, little dreams what a haunt of ancient peace and beauty he is missing. I have often landed there when staying on the river and never without a feeling that I was treading holy ground. For William Tiptaft was of the stuff whereof saints and martyrs are made, and in less tolerant days he too, I doubt not, would have gone smiling to the stake for what he knew to be the truth.

*

He and my father did not meet again until the summer of 1829 was on the wane. In the interval William Tiptaft had himself been passed through the furnace and had learnt to know the 'pangs of despised love'. For some weeks he had been deeply attached to a very amiable and devout young lady, the eldest daughter of a highly respected clergyman in the neighbourhood and a leading member of the Clerical Meeting. It was an engagement of the most serious kind in which, we are told, courtship was conducted and kisses, if any, exchanged across an open Bible. And there seemed nothing to prevent the lady from soon transferring herself and her attractions to the newly-furnished vicarage. But since that fateful conversation with my father in the garden, the young lover's views on the particularity of redemption showed signs of becoming too extreme for the lady's approval. There was a warm altercation, followed by a letter of dismissal. The father tried to accommodate the difference, but the daughter remained adamant. While smarting under this rebuff and earnestly praying for light, the text which tells how 'Lydia, a seller of purple in the city of Thyatira,' had her heart so opened by the Lord 'that she attended to the things which were spoken of Paul' (Acts 16:14) was applied with such force to the rejected lover's heart and conscience that all further doubt as to the truth of the 'hard' doctrine, which had come between him and his earthly felicity, was swept from his mind. 'I know it is a hard doctrine to receive,' he admitted years later, 'and I feel risings in my own mind against it. But when fully received in the heart, as the 17th Article describes it, it is a blessed doctrine.'

Subsequently the lady married the incumbent of a good living in the neighbourhood, and once, we learn, as William Tiptaft, no longer the respected vicar of Sutton Courtney, but a discredited itinerant preacher, was tramping along the road on foot to hold a service in some village barn, she and her husband drove past him in their carriage. But whether, comments my father, like Michal, she despised him in her heart,

C

or thought with a sigh of days gone past, is matter for con-
jecture. William Tiptaft never fell in love again, or if so, 'twas,
like Francis of Assisi, with Madam Poverty. She did not
despise his love. For her he beggared himself, and died at last
in her arms, his last field sold. For once he had left the Church,
William Tiptaft never consented to take a farthing for all his
labours in his Master's cause, and had to fall back toward the
last on the charity, or, rather let me say, on the eager benevo-
lence of devoted friends.

The narrative shall now be continued in my father's words,
written, it must be remembered, after William Tiptaft's death,
nearly forty years later.

'Those who knew William Tiptaft know that in the things
of God no minister in our day feared man less, or desired to
fear God more. His boldness and decision, where he knew and
felt himself to be right, were some of the strongest marks of his
character. Immediately, therefore, that his eyes were open to
see, and his heart touched to believe and receive the grand and
glorious truths of the gospel, and especially the fundamental
doctrine of election, as he was full of zeal and earnestness, of a
most bold, undaunted spirit, and counted the smiles of men as
dust in the balance compared with the favour of God, he began
to proclaim from the pulpit salvation by sovereign grace. He
had at that time a voice of singular loudness and power, and
his language was so plain, clear and pointed, his delivery so
warm and earnest, and he so beat down salvation by works, and
so set up salvation by grace, that a mighty stir soon began to
be made in the neighbourhood. His church, which was a very
large one, was completely thronged with hearers from all the
surrounding parishes, and the zeal, warmth and earnestness
with which he preached, new as it was to the people, sent, as it
were, an electric shock through his congregation. About this

time, as I had returned to Stadhampton, and he knew that my views were in full accordance with those which he had just embraced, he wrote me a note to ask me to come over and preach for him on a week-evening, as he had recently set up a week-evening service, and I was, from my own engagements, unable to come for a Lord's Day. Not having heard of the revolution which had taken place in his views and feelings, I was struck with the change in his language from the usual cold, stereotyped, evangelical form (as, for instance, the expression of his desire that "if I came, the Holy Spirit would enable me to preach such truth as God might bless to His people"), and accepted his invitation.

'It was about the end of the summer of that year, 1829, and, as we went into the churchyard, it was surprising to see the number of people coming along the various roads, or standing in groups waiting for the service to commence. The church soon became so filled that there was scarcely standing-room in the aisles. And of whom was the congregation made up? Almost wholly of poor men and women. Labourers were there in their smock-frocks and week-day clothes almost as if they had just come out of the fields, poor women in their cotton shawls, with a sprinkling of better-dressed people in the pews; but a thorough plain and rustic assembly had gathered together to hear a sermon on the week-day evening – an event which had not probably occurred in that church or neighbourhood since the days of the Puritans.

'He read the prayers, and especially the lesson, which was a chapter out of the epistles, with all that loudness of voice, emphasis of accent, and earnestness of manner which were always such a marked feature in him, and it seemed to thrill the whole congregation, as he roused up the sleeping echoes of the old church walls as they probably had never been roused up before.

'I shall pass by myself and my sermon, which, if I remember right, was from Isa. 45:24: "Surely, shall one say, in the Lord have I righteousness and strength", enabling me to show in whom were stored our righteousness and our strength, and that both were in Christ, and neither of them in ourselves. Though now so many years ago, I still retain some remembrance, not only of my text, but of my manner of handling it, and of the way in which I was listened to by the large congregation. As I was young in the ways and things of God, my sermon, doubtless, was neither very deep nor experimental, but I think it was a faithful exposition of the truth as far as I knew it, and most probably suited such a mixed congregation better than such a discourse as would meet my more matured judgment now.

'I slept at his house and stayed a day or two with him, during which we had much conversation on the things of God. The change in him was certainly most remarkable, and seemed to have revolutionized, as it were, his very being. He spoke and acted as one brought into a new world. The things of God were his meat and drink. The Bible, which he had not much read, now became his only book, and the doctrines of grace which he had looked on with shyness, if not fear, were uppermost in his heart and on his tongue. He never was a man to do things by halves, or calculate on consequences, I mean worldly or pecuniary consequences. If he believed a thing to be right, he did it; if wrong, no consideration could induce him to violate his conscience. If he believed a doctrine to be true, he preached it; if false, he denounced it. This made his path very clear, but one in which few can walk; for as it required strong convictions of the certainty of truth at first to attain it, so it demanded great courage, much singleness of eye, constant self-denial, and a patient bearing of the cross, which few can submit to, continually to maintain it. In some degree it was a great help to him that he had come into a new neighbourhood where he had formed no binding connections, was an incumbent, and not a curate, and thus, to a great extent, free from control by the bishop, was possessed of some personal property, and had neither wife nor children dependent on him. All these circumstances gave him a freedom of action and an independence of mind and movement which few ministers in the Church of England possess.

'But, pursuing his history, I have now to narrate an event which made at the time a considerable stir, and was indeed the chief means of bringing him out of his comparative obscurity. A Mr West, a retired medical practitioner, who had formerly practised at Abingdon, at this time resided at Sutton Courtney, and, as it appeared, was so wrought upon by the Word preached from the pulpit, and enforced by private conversation, as to embrace with zeal and warmth the doctrines of grace. It had been for many years the custom for a sermon to be preached in St Helen's, commonly called, from its size, "the great church", Abingdon, on the evening of Christmas Day, before the mayor and corporation; and as a large congregation was usually assembled, some preacher was generally chosen who it was thought could suitably address them. Chiefly through Mr West's influence, who was or had been a member of the corporation, and partly, also, as a new incumbent in the neighbourhood, the vicar of Sutton Courtney was appointed to preach it. Boldness and faithfulness, as we well know, were his marked characteristics as a preacher; but at that time these features in his character were not much known beyond the circle of his hearers at Sutton. Nothing daunted, however, by the presence of the vicar of the parish, most of the clergy of the town, and the mayor and corporation in all the dignity of mace and robes, he got into the pulpit after the vicar had, I believe, read the prayers, and to a congregation crowded in every part of one of the largest parish churches in England, delivered with all the effect of his clear, loud and ringing voice, the now well-known sermon from Matt. 1:21: "And she shall bring forth a son, and thou shalt call his name JESUS; for he shall save his people from their sins."

'Never, perhaps, did a sermon commence with a more striking opening: "I stand before you this evening as the servant of Christ, or the servant of the devil." Its effect was electric, and many remember to this day (1867) the sensation it produced on the congregation, especially the clerical and worldly part of it. Having thus opened the way, he went boldly on, and in a most plain and simple yet clear and forcible manner, brought out one by one the grand doctrines of sovereign, distinguishing grace, proving every point as he advanced it by passages from Scripture, brought together with great aptness of selection, and not too numerous or too long. The sermon, it is true, is not very deep or experimental, and yet there is such a tone of sincerity, and such warmth and life running through it, that I have thought sometimes that it was one of the best that he ever preached. Its effect was undeniable, both at the time and afterwards, for its bold, decisive statements produced such a commotion in the town of Abingdon as is rarely witnessed. Indeed, the stir that it made was so great that the enemies of truth determined to do something to allay it, and in consequence the master of the grammar school, a clergyman of the name of Hewlett, who was present at the sermon, was put the next Lord's day into the same pulpit—he being, as it was thought, a man of some ability, to answer it. This was not only contrary to the discipline of the Church of England, which forbids, under the name of "brawling", an attack upon a previous sermon in the same pulpit, but was also an unfavourable selection for their own party, as he was but a poor reasoner even on his own side of the question, and was better known as a boon companion at corporation dinners, and an excellent whist player at the card table, than as a deep theologian, or acute divine. Indeed, many of his own party were ashamed of their champion as the selected advocate of their religious views and opinions, and were surprised at seeing them entrusted to his hands. As was to be fully expected, he both misunderstood and misrepresented the doctrines advocated in the sermon which he had heard, and misquoted from memory some of its expressions; among them, if I remember right, that the preacher had called his congregation "a bundle of filthy rags". These misrepresentations (for he had the assurance to publish his discourse soon after its delivery), the general excitement produced by the original sermon, and the public attack made upon it, combined with the earnest desires expressed by many of his own congregation that he would publish his discourse, induced our friend to send it to the Press.'

The following is Tiptaft's own account of the preaching, in a letter to his brother-in-law, William Keal:

Sutton Courtney, 30 *January* 1830

'Dear Brother: Since I last wrote, I have preached in Abingdon Great Church, on Christmas evening, the only night in the year that it is lighted. I preached the truth, I trust, to a very crowded congregation, supposed to be (sitting and standing, who were able to get in) about 5,000 people. I pleased the believers, but very much displeased the carnally-minded, who were never so puzzled and confounded in their lives before. But even those who hate me and the truth acknowledge that the Bible has never before been so much read in Abingdon, or the Articles of our Church so much examined. I spoke the truth faithfully, and so as all could hear; but I had no idea that the gospel would have given so much offence. They have done nothing else since but talk about it. I allow there was much strong doctrinal matter in it, but I said no more than I fully believe.

'On the Sunday after, a clergyman preached very much against me and the doctrines which I profess. Last week he published his sermon. He misrepresents my sermon so very much that, in my own defence, I am obliged to publish it, for which there is already a great demand. It is a very long sermon, from Matt. 1:21. The clergyman who preached against me is a wine-bibber, a great card-player, and a fox-hunter. They all acknowledge if I am not right, they are sure he is not.

'The Lord is with me, for I really believe many are brought out of darkness through my preaching, and their lives manifest their faith as that which works by love and purifies the heart. It is the truth that offends and disturbs Satan's kingdom. The neighbouring clergymen, who are in the dark, say of me, "Away with such a fellow from the earth; it is not fit that he should live." Many hate, but some love me, and bless the day they first heard me. Some of the worst characters here have become decided Christians. They bring no charge against me except my views of religion; but they cannot gainsay them. Some say the Articles of our Church were buried till I brought them forth. My mind is not moved by the persecution, for I have every testimony that I am a minister of Christ, and I believe if He has a work for me to do, I shall do it, in spite of the devil and all his children. It is not coming near to the truth, it is not the letter of the gospel, that will convert men, but the Spirit.

'Make the Word of God your study. Pin your faith to no man's views. I scarcely read any other book.

'The people of Abingdon come over in large parties to hear what this troubler of Israel hath to say. Though they say all manner of evil against me falsely, they find what I say "quick and powerful, and sharper than any two-edged sword". Nature is not changed, the gospel is not changed, and Christ is not changed. What reason is there why they should not hate the truth now as much as in the time of the apostles? I never saw any fruits of my labours till I roused and disturbed the roaring lion. When, through the grace of God, I began to disturb his kingdom, I soon found that his children began to hiss; they want to know what has become of their forefathers. I came not here to judge them, but to preach the gospel. Beware of those who want to exalt man in any manner. The world and Satan hate believers. Read Paul's Epistles; they beautifully throw light upon the other Scriptures. Listen to no one who wants to mix free will and free grace, the law and the gospel; for free will is a very stronghold of Satan's. Listen to no one who talks about universal redemption. Remember Satan can transform himself into an angel of light, and his ministers into ministers of righteousness. The Pharisees hate me the most. I cut off all their rotten props, and all their fleshly devotion.

Yours very affectionately,

WILLIAM TIPTAFT'

Thus it came about that the new Vicar of Sutton Courtney was simultaneously a much-loved and a much-hated man; and in this, who dares say that his ministry does not ring true to the New Testament pattern?

8: From Church to Chapel

THIS LITTLE INTIMATE DRAMA OF A FEW OBSCURE souls doing their best by God's grace to bring their lives into harmony with the Eternal Verities takes place against the background of a world in the throes of change. Revolution abroad, the Parliamentary Reform Bill (1831–32) at home, the Roman Catholic Emancipation Act (1829), 'the daily expectation of the spreading of the cholera', the state and fate of the Established Church, are all weighing on men's minds, so that to timid souls it seemed, in the dejected words of a contemporary, 'as if the whole fabric of English and indeed of European society was trembling to the foundations'. 'Men's hearts may be said to be failing them', writes William Tiptaft late in 1831, 'for fear of what is coming upon the earth. But God's people are safe.'

In an age so incredibly heartless, brutalized and corrupt, with every public hanging, of which there were many, converted into a pandemonium; with a flagrant sinner on the throne, or only just off it; with bishops quite ready to vote for Disestablishment if they could only make sure of their life-pensions; with churches empty and beer-shops crammed, can you wonder that William Tiptaft should have come to regard the world as lying hopelessly in wickedness, and should have been moved with yearnings to call God's few chosen people out from it, as Lot had been called out of Sodom?

It was a dark hour for England, so dark, indeed, by general consent, that the more serious-minded of people were crying and groping in the dark, like frightened children, after some stable and abiding support, some 'truth of the Lord that abideth for ever'. There were those who, like that born celibate, John Henry Newman, finally came to rest upon a supposedly infallible Church; others, like his brother and Blanco White, pinned their faith on to a then presumably infallible reason; others clung the more closely to that marvellous storehouse of spiritual experience, the Bible; while a few, after long waiting, were brought out of darkness and despair by gracious manifestations of God's mercy to their souls, which made them akin to the prophets and saints of old who had been favoured with a like experience. Among the last-mentioned was the young Vicar of Sutton Courtney whose spiritual pilgrimage will at this point be continued in the words of my father as they appear in the heartfelt *Memoir* of his friend published in 1867.

'Though nearly thirty-seven years have now rolled by since that period,' writes my father, 'many can still remember the amazing stir, I may say, startling effect produced by his ministry. The cold, dead, lifeless, humdrum service of most parish churches is acknowledged even by many churchgoers, and at that period Ritualism, as it is now termed, or Puseyism, had not yet made its appearance, a little to galvanize them into a false life. There was nothing, therefore, to rouse or excite a sleepy parish or a lifeless congregation beyond the church bells or a musical choir. It was so at Sutton Courtney, which, like the rest, slept its sleep of death, until the change took place which is so obvious from his letters in the views and preaching of the new incumbent.

'The parish church of Sutton Courtney is a large building, and, besides the accommodation afforded by the old-fashioned square pews, is capable of holding a considerable congregation in its wide aisles and out-of-the-way corners. The new doctrines which he preached, in themselves so startling; the energy and power with which he enforced them; the great plainness and simplicity of language with which he clothed them — he being emphatically a poor man's preacher; his home-thrusts at besetting sins, of the poor as well as the rich; his clear, loud voice sounding through every part of the building; his bold fearlessness in hewing down error, especially Arminianism and what is called free-will, in all its shades and grades; his own evident, unmistakable conviction that what he preached was the truth of God; and the consequent earnestness of his manner and delivery — all these combined together carried with them wonderful force.

'But besides the power which evidently rested on his ministry at this remarkable period of his life, there was everything in the man himself to win esteem and affection from the people who attended it. I never knew a man who manifested less of what is called pride, either in manner or in appearance. He had nothing of that stiff, starched, clerical, donnish air which we so often see in the clergy, nor of their patronizing condescension and proud humility in their intercourse with their people. Indeed, it was not in him naturally, and he had not mixed long or intimately enough with clerical dons to acquire it. Then, as at every other period of his subsequent life, he desired to know no other distinction between man and man than such a difference as grace makes between them. A child of God was to him a child of God, and a child of the devil a child of the devil, whether he were rich or poor, educated or uneducated, lived in a good house, or dwelt in a humble cottage. Indeed, knowing that God had chosen the poor of this world to be rich in faith and heirs of the kingdom, he attached himself particularly to them; and they became his chief companions and friends. Very few of what is called the respectable part of his parish embraced his views, though at this time the lord of the manor, Mr West, whom I have already named, was most favourable to them, and advocated them with much warmth and zeal. He was also at this time, as all through his subsequent life, most kind and liberal in administering pecuniary relief to the poor and needy, and having few wants of his own, and possessing at that period a good income, kept almost open table for all in whom he could perceive the grace of God. The same divine hand which had opened his heart to believe and receive the truth, enlarged it to minister to the wants of the poor and needy of the family of God.

'He had, I must add, a most happy way of giving, and never seemed more what I may call himself, or better pleased, than in doing it. He generally carried his money loose in his waistcoat pocket, and rarely passed a beggar without giving him something. Indeed, at Abingdon, many years after this period of his life, as I have myself seen, he was continually as if waylaid by boys and poor people, who begged of him as he passed by, and rarely in vain. I write nothing about him but what I myself was personally witness of, as we frequently saw each other at this period; and indeed I may add that I was almost the only clergyman in the neighbourhood who cleaved to him, for all his former evangelical friends were frightened at what they considered his new and extravagant views; and he felt as much separated from them in spirit as they were from him now in person. But from the similarity of our views and feelings we seemed more closely drawn together, and as we lived only six or seven miles apart, often saw one another, he coming over to visit me, or I spending a day or two with him.

'But in the autumn of 1830, a circumstance brought us into closer habits of intimacy. In September it pleased the Lord to lay on me His afflicting hand. I had overworked myself in my parish, and having taken a severe cold, and increased it by going out one evening to my lecture at the school-room, was quite laid aside and unable to preach. My friend hearing of my illness came over to see me several times, and rendered me

[77]

what help he could in my week lectures; but finding my health did not improve, kindly invited me to come and stay with him for a few weeks for change of air, as Sutton was drier and warmer than Stadhampton. This invitation I willingly accepted, and went to his house November 4, meaning to return home in a few weeks. He was, however, so kind and hospitable, and we got on so well together, that I was easily persuaded to remain with him the whole of the winter, especially as I still continued tender, not being able to leave the house all through December and January. During those winter months, nothing could exceed his affectionate kindness and attention, waiting upon me like a brother, bringing to me my breakfast in bed and afterwards assisting me to shave myself. We spent the morning alone in our own rooms, he giving up to me his airy and cheerful drawing-room; but in the evening we generally sat together, and either read the Bible, or conversed, I think I may say almost always, on something connected with the concerns of eternity; for I may add that it was a solemn period with me at that time, with many searchings of heart and prayers to the Lord as regarded my own state; for eternity was brought near, and I was made to see and feel, that nothing short of divine manifestations, and Christ revealed to the heart, could bear the soul up in the trying hour.

'At that period of his life he was singularly frank and free both naturally and spiritually, more so, perhaps, than afterwards, when from having been often deceived in men, he had become more cautious in expressing his thoughts and opinions; and as we were well agreed, for the most part, in divine things, I probably knew as much of his mind and past history as, or perhaps more than, most of his friends and acquaintances.[1]

'In the beginning of February 1831 I was able to leave the

[1] Tiptaft's esteem of Philpot is expressed in a letter written at this time: 'I have spent this winter very pleasantly, being blessed with

[78]

house, and take a walk under a sunny wall where he would accompany me and suit his pace to mine; and as strength mercifully came with the advancing season, I was enabled to go to the church, and hear him preach. What a congregation he then had, and made up chiefly of poor people, and, what is not very usual, the men much preponderating in number over the women. This, however, may be easily accounted for by the distances whence they came, which of course the men were more easily enabled to accomplish. I do not think I had heard him preach before this, and therefore take the present opportunity of recording my impression of his ministry at this period of his life. I cannot say, then, that he had much of what is called eloquence of language, at least to an educated ear, if that mean sublimity of thought and beauty of expression; but he had much of what Richard Cecil defines true eloquence to be, "vehement simplicity", and, above all, that thorough conviction in his own heart of the truths which he preached with so much simple vehemence, and without which all eloquence is but theatrical oratory, and for the most part utterly powerless to either sinner or saint.

'About this time he became acquainted with a Mr Bulteel, then curate of St Ebbe's parish in the city of Oxford. Mr Bulteel had for some years embraced the doctrines of grace, and preached them with much fervour of mind and strength of expression. This was a new sound at the learned University, and a thing almost unheard of, that a Fellow and tutor of one of the colleges, for such he was when he first began to preach, should embrace so thoroughly, and above all proclaim so

such a valuable friend as Philpot for my companion. He is a very highly gifted man, but he desires to present his body a living sacrifice unto Christ. He is delicate in health and is affected with a pain in his chest. He will continue with me during the winter, I hope, for his conversations are very profitable to me, and we see eye to eye in almost every point; so there is no jarring and arguments.'

boldly, the obnoxious doctrines of the Calvinistic creed. His church was crowded with hearers, and among them were seen many of the University students, and now and then a master of arts, myself being one of them, some of whom became his attached and regular hearers. As a master of arts (for every ordained master of arts preaches once, according to his turn, before the University), it fell to Mr Bulteel early in 1830 to preach before that learned body; and true to his principles he took for his text 1 Cor. 2:12, from which he delivered a bold and faithful discourse, distinctly and clearly advocating the doctrines of grace. I need hardly say that to wake up the echoes of St Mary's Church, and rouse from their calm repose the minds of proctors, doctors, heads of houses, learned professors, and the grand assembly of University dons, who, besides the general gathering of masters of arts and the under-graduate students, form the congregation, by bold statements of Calvinistic doctrine was no slight task to accomplish. But Mr Bulteel preached an able and faithful sermon, and though he contended strongly for free-grace, as opposed to free-will, yet kept clear of any offensive statements. The sermon, however, caused much sensation, and Mr Bulteel felt himself called upon to publish it. This called forth a reply from Dr Burton, the chaplain to the bishop, producing a controversy between them which made some little noise at the time, but which it is not worth while further to notice.[1]

[1] 'Dr Burton's reply to Bulteel', we read elsewhere, 'had shown him to be excitable and not always able to command himself.' Dr Burton had succeeded Bishop Lloyd as Regius Professor of Divinity at Oxford, but died in 1836, under circumstances which that genial gossip, the Rev. T. Mozley, to whom I owe the above quotation, thus relates: 'Feeling not quite well, Dr Burton went to Ewelme for a few days' rest, took a walk in the fields, met a dissenting farmer, who told him — a Regius Professor of Divinity — that he did not preach the gospel, had a warm argument with him, came home in a fever and died in a few days.' (*Reminiscences,* Vol. I, p. 350.)

'Of course all this deeply interested our friend, and led to a closer acquaintance with Mr Bulteel, which soon began to bear fruit. They were both young and healthy, vigorous in mind and body, and full of zeal and warmth, which were roused instead of being damped by the general opposition made to their views and preaching. Tiptaft had not at that time that wisdom, discernment and caution which he manifested in after years; and as the doctrines of grace had taken such possession of his soul, his heart and house were alike open to all who advocated them, and were willing to make sacrifices for them. Mr Bulteel was a Devonshire man, and being of a good family had many connections and friends in that county. He therefore proposed to his friend that they should go down together on a kind of preaching excursion, not confining themselves to Church of England places of worship, but to proclaim the Gospel wherever a door might be opened in chapels, rooms, private houses, or the open air. Our friend's mind at that time had become much shaken about the Church of England, and this made him all the more willing to accompany Mr Bulteel, and take a part with him. Indeed, I am not sure whether the original proposal did not emanate from him.'

This preaching tour is described for us in a letter sent to the Keals at that time and dated 27 July 1831:

'My dear Brother: Through the mercy and goodness of God, I am again quietly settled at Sutton after my two months' tour in the West of England. I arrived on Friday, 15 July, and left Bulteel with his wife and child in Devon, for I could not conscientiously leave my own flock any longer; for during my absence they were left almost without food, as I could not get a minister of Christ for love or money.

'Soon after I wrote to you we left Somerset for Belle Vue,

near Plymouth, and began to preach in that neighbourhood. We stopped about ten days in the vicinity of Plymouth. Bulteel preached in the large church at Plymouth, which was also offered to me; and I should have accepted it, had I remained another Sunday. When Bulteel preached there it was crowded to excess. We preached also in the open air, and in what churches we could obtain, to the great annoyance of the Church clergy. They consulted together whether they could not put us into the stocks. Of course they called upon my Lord Bishop to restrain us. We were the more offensive because multitudes would flock together to hear us.

'After we left Plymouth, we travelled along the southern coast of Devon, and preached in several of the principal towns. We both preached. Consequently we kept our hearers standing nearly two hours, and sometimes longer. We preached fifteen nights out of eighteen in the open air, and the numbers that gathered together surprised us; but the novelty of it, and the size of the towns were much the cause. I will mention a few of the towns: Modbury, Kingsbridge, Dartmouth, Brixham, Torquay, Teignmouth, Totnes, Exmouth, etc., etc. We had generally a table to stand upon. I preached upon the quays, as many of the places were by the sea, or had a large river running by them. We were not much molested, considering the offensive truths we preached, and the numbers of the vilest characters amongst our hearers. But we were called every name that was applied to Christ and the first preachers of the gospel, and we were pelted with a few stones and dirt, etc. But, upon the whole, we had but little to bear for our great and gracious Master. We preached twice at Teignmouth, and twice at Exeter, in the open air. A constable and a magistrate came the second night at Exeter, but we regarded them not, and they dared not touch us, nor could they prevent us, for we had a message for thousands.

'Our flesh rebelled much against the work; but I am sure nothing would excite a neighbourhood more than faithful preachers standing up in that way. But they must preach the finished work of Christ, or little effect in any way will be manifested. We were followed from place to place by several, and they who were taught of God knew the sound. We were much refreshed by conversations with God's dear people, who were chiefly amongst the poor, and they, alas! poor creatures, were almost without shepherds. Great darkness prevails, and very few preach the fulness of the gospel. That part of Devon in which we were is as dark as Rutland, and almost as void of true ministers. Many of God's dear people showed us great kindness, and those who received us we called Jasons; for they certainly had to bear a cross. Mr Synge, of Buckeridge House, near Teignmouth, was very kind to us. He stood by us twice in the open air at Teignmouth. We took up our abode with him, and he sent us in his carriage to Totnes, and met us again at Exeter, and stood by us again. May the Lord reward him! He is a man of property, and cousin to your curate.

'I could not, in one or two letters, say all that you might desire to know about our journey. But the great question is, Who were converted; and who were comforted? We heard of convictions which were very striking. If no blossom there will be no fruit, but of course we knew but little of the effect of our preaching, as we started away directly, and went immediately to another place. But many could testify of our preaching that it was good for them to be there. We had a very great number of ministers of all sorts to hear us. Some said we were mad, some said that we were good men, some said that we deceived the people, some mocked, and others said that they should like to hear us again. Very many, both rich and poor, wondered how we dared preach everywhere and anywhere, and they wanted to know what our diocesans will say. I have heard nothing from mine, although I am sure he knows of it. Bulteel is to return for Sunday next. I do not think that he has heard from his bishop. We are both indifferent how our diocesans may act. If they turn us out of the Church of England, we shall see our way clear; for we both think, that if a mother ever had a daughter, our Established Church is one of Rome's. Bulteel can easily be removed, but they will find difficulty in removing me, as I am an incumbent. I think they will be afraid of interfering with Bulteel, as his name is so well known, and the poor Establishment is tottering to its very basis. As I mentioned before, the canons cannot prove us guilty, and the Scriptures are on our side. My desire is to do the Lord's work, and I shall not stop (D.V.) in bearing a testimony for Jesus, concerning those precious truths I know for my own comfort, whenever I have an opportunity.'

The Bishop of Salisbury, Tiptaft's diocesan, though ready enough, as we shall see later on, to threaten him with prosecution after he had left the Church, now made no sign. But Henry Bulteel had his licence withdrawn by his Bishop, and, refusing to be silenced, after preaching for a time in his own garden, built himself a chapel behind Pembroke College, Oxford.

It is all rather pathetic, to read of these ardent but inexperienced young enthusiasts going forth full of zeal to convert the world, soon coming up against the world's massive scepticism or indifference, and in the end falling back upon an obscure ministry to a handful of humble but spiritually-minded souls. They learnt from their efforts at least as much as they taught. The lack of adequate response to their passionate appeals drove them more and more firmly to believe in the existence of a chosen and predestined people, disposing them, like the prophet of old, to attribute their failure to God's design. 'Therefore they could not believe, because that Esaias said again, He hath blinded their eyes, and hardened their heart; that they should not see with their eyes, nor understand with their heart, and be converted, and I should heal them' (John 12:39, 40). In some such strain do we find William Tiptaft writing when the first excitement of the tour was over, 'We have found the spirit of the world reigning much wherever we have been. All seem to be seeking their own. There are very few that have grace enough to come out of a world lying in wickedness. The Dissenters generally are very worldly.'

At one time he seems to have cherished the hope that many more clergy would follow him in the secession on which he was now almost resolved, and that the Church of England would totter to its fall.[1] In fact, only a few months later, Arnold of Rugby was to enunciate his well-known verdict, 'The Church as it now stands no human power can save.' But this would have brought small comfort to William Tiptaft, unless accompanied with a general religious revival. Disillusion followed on disillusion, till we find him exclaiming in despair, that true religion seemed nearly as scarce as snowballs in summer or roses at Christmas.

But his worst disappointment, in which my father also shared, a disappointment he could hardly bear to speak of, was the defection of his own familiar friend and fellow-labourer, on whom the meagre harvest of the tour had produced calamitous results. As late as September 1831, Bulteel had stayed with him, and preached in Abingdon market-place to two or three thousand people. Subsequently he had gone up to London, fallen under the spell of Edward Irving, then at the height of his popularity, and been persuaded not only that all

---

[1] According to my father, see *Secession from the Church of England Defended* (7th edition London, 1887) p. 8, between forty and fifty ordained clergymen in various parts of England quitted the Established Church in the years 1830–35.

men might be pardoned, but were already pardoned, and that Christ had only been kept from sin by the power of the Holy Spirit.

Writing to the Keals about this Tiptaft says: 'My old friend Bulteel and I can have no communion. He holds the doctrine of universal pardon, is now distinguished for universal charity, and accuses God's children, who hold the doctrine of particular redemption, as having a bad spirit. Christ was accused of having one, and so must His household. He has a large chapel building. He and I scarcely ever meet, for we differ widely, though it is reported in distant places that I have fallen into his errors.' Mr Bulteel afterwards renounced his errors and confessed that he had been misled, but we hear no more of him. The rupture was complete.

In the meanwhile my father, having entrusted his parish to the 'seasonable help' of the Rev. Charles Brenton, had left Sutton Courtney vicarage as soon as the spring was well advanced, in order to complete his convalescence in his mother's house at Walmer. Passing through London he consulted Sir William Knighton, the King's physician, who, having decided that he was suffering from 'exhaustion of the vital energy', advised a full year's complete rest, a prescription which, as it turned out, was easier to order than to obey. Yet, well or ill, Tiptaft and he maintained their fellowship in the Lord by a constant exchange of letters.

It was characteristic of William Tiptaft that, as soon as he realized that he could not keep his living with a good conscience, he did not hesitate, but acted with promptitude. So that when my father was unexpectedly recalled to his parish at the end of 1831, his friend's secession was already six weeks old, and the walls of the chapel he had decided to build at Abingdon were nearly ready for the roof. He had received several offers to settle elsewhere, but had declined them all on the ground that those who made them could afford to pay a minister, which his own poor peasants could not.

On 10 November 1831 he had thus begun a long and reasoned letter to the Bishop of Salisbury, his diocesan:

'I trust that you will not be displeased, because I do not address you with the high and usual appellation, when I assure you that I refrain from doing so with no personal disrespect to you, but for conscience' sake, as being expressly contrary to the plain and simple command of my Lord Jesus Christ. The subject of this letter is to me of great and serious importance, and has caused me much anxiety and consideration; but after frequent prayer to the Lord for His direction, I feel constrained to resign my living, as I cannot conscientiously discharge the duties thereof.'

The bishop having accepted his resignation, William Tiptaft went up to London to complete the necessary formalities before a notary towards the end of November. On the last day of that month he published his Letter to the Bishop, and thought he had done with him. The Letter sold like wildfire. Three thousand copies were soon disposed of, and a new edition called for. In all nine editions were printed. Newspapers inserted it in full, and a bookseller published it without asking his leave. His indictment against the Church of England is formulated under fourteen objections, but since the case is put so much more forcibly by my father in his letter to the Provost of Worcester College (see Appendix), William Tiptaft's manifesto need not detain us.

The chapel at Abingdon was ready for occupation and was to be formally opened on 25 March, when William Tiptaft was astounded by the receipt of the following letter:

14 *March* 1832

'Rev. Sir: It has come to the knowledge of the Bishop of

Salisbury that you are itinerating within his Lordship's diocese, preaching doctrines inconsistent with the principles of the Established Church, of which you have been ordained a member, in direct violation of the canons made for the governance of the ministers of that Church. I am therefore instructed by his Lordship to require you to desist from such practices within his Lordship's diocese, and to inform you, that if this requisition be not complied with, legal proceedings will be commenced against you.

I am, Rev. Sir,

Your very obedient servant,

J. L. ALFORD,

Proctor, Salisbury'

The reader, who may be presumed to know the sort of man that William Tiptaft was much better than the Bishop of Salisbury and his advisers appear to have done, will not be surprised at the uncompromising tenor of his rejoinder, dated 19 March 1832. It is too long to quote, but two sentences will give the gist of it.

1. 'In the language of that honest servant, Micaiah, "As the Lord liveth, what the Lord saith unto me, that will I speak"' (1 Kings 22:14).

2. 'If my great Master has a work for me to do in His vineyard, He will not allow all the powers in earth and hell to prevent it.'

Still egged on by his advisers the Bishop affirms in his second letter of 22 March that resignation of a Church living does not operate as a renunciation of holy orders, or exonerate from the observance of the ecclesiastical law, as applicable to the clergy of the Church of England. And again he threatens 'hostile measures'.

On 27 March William Tiptaft again replies at length. Well

aware that the Ecclesiastical Court is 'the worst of all Courts and something like a porch to a prison', he repeats that he intends to preach as hitherto, until the Bishop or others show him by the Word of God that he is wrong in so doing. If the Bishop had any love and life in his soul, his treatment of him (William Tiptaft) would not be so *unlike* Paul's advice to Bishops Timothy and Titus, who had no Ecclesiastical Court nor Proctors.

The Bishop now changes his ground and instead of threatening his late subordinate for preaching doctrines inconsistent with the principles of the Church of England, a position which it would have been difficult to establish, now arraigns him for preaching in unconsecrated places.

The letter is worth preserving, just as a thunderbolt that has gone astray, or an old posting blunderbuss is exhibited under glass in a museum. The Bishop and his friends must have known that they were bluffing. Even a century ago a prosecution in the Ecclesiastical Court would have raised such a storm as they would not soon have heard the last of.

Sarum, 2 *April* 1832

'Rev. Sir: I regret that I am obliged to repeat to you that you entirely misunderstood the tenor of my letters. It is not the desire of the Bishop of Salisbury to prosecute you on account of your religious opinions, but merely to prevent your violating the law by preaching in unconsecrated places within his lordship's diocese. I must repeat also, that you cannot by the aid of any authority legally or effectually renounce your orders, or your connection with the Church of England, and that consequently you are still, and will hereafter be, bound not to offend against the laws of that Church, notwithstanding your secession from it.

'One of these laws is, that its ministers shall not preach in any other place than a consecrated Church or Chapel. You declare your intention to break that law. And the Bishop, as your diocesan, admonishes you not to do so, and at the same time intimates to you, that if you persist in your determination, he will be compelled, in the exercise of his duty, to enforce your observance of that law by the usual proceedings.

'I trust I have now been sufficiently explicit to prevent any future communications to the Bishop of the character of your last two letters, both of which, I must take the liberty to say, are libellous, not only as they relate to his lordship individually, but also to the clergy of his lordship's diocese generally.

I am, Rev. Sir,

Your very obedient servant,

J. L. ALFORD'

The only reply which William Tiptaft made to this communication was to publish it. Together with his original letter, his correspondence with the Bishop, and a lengthy preface, it made up a nice little pamphlet which for several years enjoyed a considerable circulation, and is still, I believe, on sale. The Edition from which I quote is the fourth, dated 1850. After that they left him severely alone. The Bishop threw over his reckless advisers and fell back on the worldly-wise counsel of old Gamaliel.

Tiptaft continued to preach to overflowing congregations in a borrowed chapel at Sutton Courtney, and elsewhere in the neighbourhood. 'I have been preaching in various places,' he tells his brother-in-law, 'and to large concourses of people. One of the effects of the Bishop's interference is that he has been an excellent trumpeter for me, and the newspapers, still continuing to make their remarks upon me, cause many to come and hear "the babbler" out of curiosity.' Some time later he heard in a roundabout way that the Bishop thought favourably and spoke well of him. 'Nevertheless he remarked, that I had not spoken very gently of him.'

In due course, the chapel at Abingdon, to build which Tiptaft had sold an ancestral field, was opened, and within its red-brick walls he ministered to the Lord and nurtured His people until his death more than thirty years later.

9: 'I must see my way clear'

STADHAMPTON, IN THE MISTY VALLEY OF THE THAME, has little to recommend it on the score of salubrity, for no one who has ever lived upon the gault can forget what a raw and depressing climate it engenders. 'I believe', wrote my father long after he had left it, 'that the damp air and soil of Stadham, where I was for nearly seven years in the Church of England, have affected my health up to the present hour.' Two claims, however, has the place on our present sympathy and interest. First, it is close to Chalgrove Field, the consecrated spot where, in the early days of the Civil War when Charles I and his Court were at Oxford, John Hampden, that 'heroic idealist' as Prof. Trevelyan has called him, received his death-wounds from Prince Rupert's carbineers. Secondly, it was the birth-place, and will always remain associated with the memory, of the foremost of the Puritan divines, Dr John Owen, whom Cromwell, when the tables had been turned, made Dean of Christ Church in that very Oxford, and whom my father in after-years singled out for his warm admiration, calling him 'a writer of great depth and feeling, a master in Israel', and picking out choice morsels from his 'Discourses' to fill up odd corners in the *Gospel Standard*.[1]

That he should have come to regard with such especial favour a leading light of the contemned Puritans, shows what a revolution was taking place in his views and affections even before he left the Church of England, which at that time in one of its Offices still branded the followers of Cromwell as

[1] See his article on Dr Owen's *Meditations and Discourses on the Glory of Christ. Reviews,* Vol. II, p. 88.

[92]

'men of Belial'. During his early years at Stadhampton he was, in fact, being torn between two loyalties. Until his call by grace in 1827, he tells us, he idolized the English Church and thought a word against her treason. Even later he loved her still and was able to blind himself to her many inconsistencies. It was only after a bitter struggle within his own soul that his passionate adoration of Christ finally overcame his devotion to the Church in which he had been reared. The psychologists very rightly insist on 'the expulsive power of a new affection'. A single heart – a truly single heart, cannot serve two masters. Or as the hymn-writer puts it,

> God requires pure desires,
> All the heart, or nothing.

In other words, if the human spirit fixes too many of its tentacles upon the Temple, it will have too few left for Him who is greater than the Temple.

For illustration, the Roman Catholic Professor De Sanctis in trying to explain why E. B. Pusey did not follow his friend, John Henry Newman, to Rome, asks naïvely, 'What affective necessity could bring about the conversion of Edward Pusey, whose soul was already centred upon the Anglican religion, upon which he lavished all the love he had felt for his dead wife, and the divine origin of which he never doubted?'[1]

Dr Pusey, it will be remembered, was one of the youthful company who were ordained by Bishop Lloyd on the same day as my father. That very evening he confided to his diary, 'If I do not dedicate all my strength to it (the Church); if I do not exert every power to purify my heart and improve my mind, as may most tend to advance His kingdom, I shall have broken my faith solemnly pledged, be a deserter, a renegade, a worse

[1] *Religious Conversion* (1927), p. 111.

than slothful servant'. How well, and to what purpose that pledge was kept, has been detailed in four volumes by his friend, Canon Liddon.

At the date of his ordination my father might almost have written the passage above quoted. That you may judge how far in the course of the next few years he was to be carried beyond that standpoint, pray read the following avowal, dated March 1842.

'In truth I find religion to be a very different thing from what I once thought it. There was a time when, in all sincerity, I was looking up to my spirituality and heavenly-mindedness, as evidences of my standing, instead of being a poor needy suppliant and starving petitioner for a word or a smile from the Lord Himself. It seemed more as if my spirituality were to take me up to Christ, than that my miserable poverty and nakedness were qualifications to bring Christ down to me. But all these idols have tumbled into ruins.'

If we follow such records as he has left us of his experiences at Stadhampton, we may actually watch them tumbling.

'When persons breathed a word against the Church of England formerly,' he writes in February 1840, 'I felt the bitterest enmity rise up, and I wanted to put them down, stop their mouths, or keep them in any way from broaching a subject so painful to the flesh. But still light would break in and work in my conscience. The burdens of a liturgy and the awful lies I was compelled to tell a heart-searching God pressed me sore. There was no use my fleeing to this or that explanation. I stood before a holy God and told Him with lying lips that a senseless babe was born of water and the Holy Ghost, when I knew the blessed Spirit had no more regenerated the child than He had regenerated the font. I thanked Him for taking a "dear brother" to Himself, who I knew died under His eternal wrath. But some might say "How did you know either the one, or the other?" How did I know there was a God at all, but by faith in His Word? And by the same faith that I believed in Him, did I believe that His enemies were not His friends, nor carnal children living members of the true Vine. I twisted and turned every way, but I was here held fast. It is a lie, and the worst of lies, as being a lie unto God.'

In my attempted portrait of William Tiptaft I have had to refer incidentally to my father's critical illness and nervous breakdown in September 1830, of which he has said, 'I once made great attempts to be holy, and was getting on pretty well, with, however, some terrible inward pull-backs sometimes, till the winter of 1830–31, when it all went to wrack and ruin.' His friend was away at the time 'troubling Israel' down in Rutland, and he was all alone in a comfortless farm-house with only an overworked old woman to look after him. 'Death stared me in the face,' he tells us, 'and I used to count how many months I had to live. How I used then to roll about on my midnight bed, with scarcely a hope in my soul; and turned my face to the wall, like good old Hezekiah. In that illness I was made to see and feel that something more than doctrine and knowledge of the truth was required to bear up the soul in the solemn hour. Not that I was not blessed and favoured in the first part of my illness; for I well remember that as I lay very ill in bed on my birthday (13 Sept.) I was so happy in my soul that I said, "This is the happiest birthday that I ever had". But afterwards I was much tried in my mind and brought low both in body and mind, and led down into the chambers of imagery, as I had never been before.'

The following passage from a sermon on eternal life will throw further light on his state of mind at this period. 'When in the Church of England, I had one day to bury a little child, one of the sweetest children in the poorer walks of life that I ever knew. The funeral being a little delayed, I stood at the grave till they brought the corpse for me to bury. I was very poorly in body but favoured in soul; I looked into the grave, and felt, "Oh, how sweet to lie down there! I never shall be happy in this life; it is but a scene of affliction and sorrow, and I never shall have a body free from sickness and sin till I have a glorified body". How sweet to look forward to a happy eternity! What a glorious prospect, when realized by faith – eternal bliss in the presence of God; joy for evermore in that happy, eternal home!'

'Slow and sluggish,' he writes elsewhere of the body,[1] a constant clog to the soul; chained down to the dull clods of clay amongst which it toils and labours; wearied with a few miles' walk to chapel, or with sitting an hour on the same seat; with eyes, ears, mouth, all inlets and outlets to evil; tempting and tempted; galloping to evil and crawling to good; with its shattered nerves, aching joints, panting lungs, throbbing head, and all the countless ills that flesh is heir to; what is this poor earthly frame fit for but to drop into the grave, and be buried out of sight till the glorious resurrection morn?'

It has already been mentioned how my father, having entrusted his parish to the Rev. Charles Brenton, a young Oxford graduate of Oriel College, left the hospitable vicarage of Sutton Courtney, and went to complete his convalescence at Walmer, in his mother's house. He had not been long there, however, when, as we learn from the earliest of his preserved letters, complaints began to reach him from his parishioners that they received no comfort from Mr Brenton's preaching, in reply to which he urges them to be earnest in prayer that the Lord may speak in him and by him to the hearts of His people.

Writing to his friend Tiptaft, he says in this connection, under the date 7 September 1831:

[1] *Reviews,* Vol. I, p. 39.

'I hope you will go over to Stadham, before you go away for a time. Can't you go over the day this reaches you? it is the usual lecture-night. I could wish that Brenton had more the gift of preaching, and could speak more to the comfort and edification of the people. His sermons are too dry and abstract, too much the reflections of his own mind, and need simplicity of statement and application. They are good and true as far as they go, but they want that energy and speaking to the heart, and suiting it to the cares and wants of the hearers, which make preaching profitable. They require too much attention to follow, and a mind in some degree imbued with the truth, and able to catch it when obscurely stated, to be generally useful. I am thankful, however, for the seasonable help the Lord has sent me in him, and feel a confidence in him which I could not have done in another. Besides which, I trust the Lord will teach him, and apply the truth with such power to his heart, that he will be constrained to speak it with power to others. Preaching without book, too, will, I think, be useful in leading him to greater simplicity of statement, and bringing him out of that essay style into which he has fallen. I fear I shall not be able to comply with the wishes of the Stadham people in taking a part of the service. In the first place, I need rest, especially during the winter, when each cold affects my chest; and, secondly, if I were sufficiently strong, I should not think it right to interfere with Brenton. I have left him there to be in my place, which he has kindly consented to occupy; and if I were to return, of course the whole would seem to revert to me, and he be only my assistant. I think it best to leave him in sole charge, and am thankful I can do it so much to my own satisfaction. His visits and conversation, and his lectures, perhaps may be more profitable than his preaching, and it may lead the children of God to pray for him, and so be beneficial to their souls and his.'

D

To one of his parishioners he gives the following advice:

'The advice which I would give to the children of God at Stadham, etc., is to search the Scriptures much for themselves, and be much in prayer for themselves and for each other. If they cannot derive that benefit which they would wish from their present minister, let them pray much for him, that God would teach him, and speak in him and by him to their souls. You may call to mind that when I left Stadham for a little while in May 1830, the children of God were much in prayer that when I returned I might be enabled to preach more to their comfort and edification. I think they acknowledged at the time that the Lord, in a measure at least, heard their prayers. Let them now pray in the same way for their present minister, and the Lord will hear and answer. I really do not know where I could get a more satisfactory person. You all know how much trouble and anxiety it cost me, when Mr T—— left, to procure the aid of any one even from Sunday to Sunday, and scarcely any except my dear friend Mr G—— preached to the edification of the saints.'

Towards the end of September my father left Walmer for Petersfield (Hants.), meeting William Tiptaft in London on the way, when, we may be sure, the burning question of secession was again most gravely discussed in all its bearings. He was still at Petersfield, undecided as yet where to find a sheltered spot for the winter, when Charles Brenton's unexpected secession[1]

---

[1] The occasion of his leaving the Church of England was the reading of the burial service over a drunkard. This man had been parish clerk for forty years, but during his last illness had so terrified his nurse with his oaths and imprecations that she could hardly stay in the room with him. He died in black despair, calling down curses on all parsons, Philpot amongst them. In order that he might not again be called upon to perform the 'terrible task' of proclaiming to all and sundry that 'it hath pleased Almighty God of His great mercy to take his soul unto Himself', Brenton quitted the Established Church.

recalled him to his parish. Once there, he found himself so wonderfully strengthened for his work, that he concluded that he was not meant to leave it. There followed more than three years of deep exercise of soul and grievous indecision, of letting 'I dare not' wait upon 'I would', during which he salved his conscience as best as he could by delegating to an assistant such parts of his duty as he could not conscientiously perform himself.

There can be no doubt that after his long stay and intimate converse with William Tiptaft at Sutton Courtney, and the months of rest in his mother's house at Walmer, when he made his first real acquaintance at *The Refuge* in Deal with Henry Fowler, John Kent and other kindred souls, my father came back to Stadhampton in a very different frame of mind. His difficulties were not lessened, were indeed increased, but he had more health and strength and vital experience to cope with them. Fortunately from this point onwards some of his letters have been preserved which throw light upon his state of mind. Of almost all of them the burden is, 'I must see my way clear'. 'Nothing short of an answer that the Lord will be my guide, so that I might see the pillar of cloud going before me, will ever induce me to leave my present post.' Again, 'I am praying to be delivered from a carnal system, but my way out at present seems hedged up. I can't move just when and as I please, but must wait for the pillar and the cloud.'

Considering his state of health, one can well understand his hesitation. To leave the Church of England involved resigning both his Fellowship and his living, and going forth into the world without any apparent means of subsistence. His mother on her limited income could not support him in idleness, while his health debarred him from regular occupation as a schoolmaster, or tutor. To unfrock himself meant, in his own words, 'parting for truth's sake with the kindest friends after the flesh, as well as with all my prospects in life, an independent income, good name and respectability'.

And yet, on the other hand: 'Oh! how the sacrament so-called used to gall me! At the head knelt my carnal Pharisaical squire, with his pleasure-loving, God-hating wife, who was so filled with enmity against me that she would never hear me preach. I was compelled to tell them individually and personally that Christ died for them and shed His blood for their sins (I believing all the while in particular redemption), of which I put the elements into their hands, saying, "Take, eat this," etc. Lower down knelt a man generally suspected of having once committed a murder, and near him the most hardened Pharisee I ever knew in my life, whose constant reply to my attempted warnings, etc., was "I dare say it be as you says". I was so cut up and condemned that at last I could not do it, and employed an assistant to perform the whole, but then I had to kneel down with these characters, which was as bad; and so I found myself completely hedged in and driven from every refuge, till at last, like an animal hunted down to a rock by the sea-side, I had only one escape, which was to leap into the water, which bore me up and afforded me a sweet deliverance from my persecutors.'

From then until the end of his life, my father, while surrounded by devoted friends of his own austere faith, had to submit to the persecution and obloquy which the human herd invariably visits on those who separate themselves from it, and presume to differ in conduct and opinion. True prophets are born to be stoned. It is God's inscrutable will. Had he lived when that great herd known as the Roman Church was in power, he would no doubt have been sent to the stake, as was his namesake John Philpot in the reign of Queen Mary, for refusing to adore the sacred elements. As it was, that less powerful herd, the Church of England, did its best to victimize him by all the expedients in its power. 'Besides my own,' he records, 'I had but one pulpit open to me in the Establishment in the neighbourhood, and that was more as an accommodation for the person, than love to the truth, as he preached it and, I believe, knew it not. I and another clergyman, a notorious adulterer, almost a *taurus publicus* in his parish, were the only persons the bishop refused to bow to at his visitation.'

Bishop Lloyd by this time was no more, and Dr Bagot, a much less able man, had succeeded him as Bishop of Oxford. On the whole he treated his wayward subordinate with leniency, if not politeness. A complaint was lodged with him that my father from the pulpit had condemned his fellow-clergy for taking out shooting-licences. It found its way, I gather, into the episcopal waste-paper basket. He reprimanded him for employing an assistant without his leave, but took no further steps against him. In 1833, for reasons which appear below, my father deliberately omitted sending up any candidates from his parish for confirmation, quite expecting to have his licence withdrawn. Indeed, he would have welcomed it, as a way out of his difficulties. The wary bishop made no sign, anticipating perhaps that, given rope enough, the offender would perform his own execution, as in the event he did.

'At the last confirmation which I attended,' wrote my father a few years later, 'a waggon was sent from one parish to convey to the ceremony all the young persons who were to be confirmed. And how did these youths and girls, who had just been called "the servants of God", and "all whose sins were said to have been forgiven them", conduct themselves on their way home? The youths, as I was assured by an eye-witness, amused themselves by pulling off the shawls, and untying with loud merriment the bonnets of the girls, who in their turn affected to be angry, though they showed by their smiles that they were inwardly pleased, with the rude jokes and romping of the boys. If we take the text given us, 1 John 3:8-10, as our rule, instead of calling such as these "the servants of God", would it not be the greater truth to have called them "the servants of the devil"?'[1]

*

About the time that my father was deeply exercised about his ministry as an Anglican clergyman, he found a keen sympathizer in the person of Mr Joseph Parry, a spiritually-minded young farmer, who was supporting, not without difficulty, a little Baptist chapel which had recently been opened at Allington, a retired hamlet in the very heart of Wiltshire, at the foot of the downs and some six miles from Devizes. The account which follows, though contained in a letter written by Parry to my mother nearly forty years after the event, owes its interest to the fact that it gives the only existing description by an eye-witness of my father's ministry while in the Church of England:

'Before I knew Mr Philpot in the flesh, my mind became impressed in a most remarkable manner, through a conversation which I had with your late dear uncle, William Tiptaft, in the year 1832, relative to the state of soul-experience through which dear Mr Philpot, then in the Church of England, was passing. I was told that he was so tried and exercised by fears that he was doing wrong in remaining where he was, his conscience was so burdened with the forms and ceremonies he had to attend to, that he had, moreover, such a weak chest, that if ever he saw his way to leave the Establishment he would be unable to take a large place or congregation, and that it was such a trial to his weak state and troubled mind as few persons

[1] *Secession from the Church of England defended.* (7th Edition, 1887.) Preface, v. p. 94.

had ever gone through. After relating to me very many of his deep soul-exercises, and telling me into what a humble, sweet state of mind he was brought down, Mr Tiptaft said, "I believe the Lord has so prepared him, that he would be satisfied with ever so humble a residence, provided it were dry, not damp, and were wind-tight and water-tight, with a few poor sensible sinners to preach to, rather than remain with the fetters he has now to keep him in bondage. He said to me the other day, 'Tiptaft, all that I can now feelingly say is, Lord, I am oppressed, undertake for me!'"

'This conversation made such a deep and lasting impression on my mind that I could never get rid of it. It gave me some little encouragement to hope that, as dear Mr Philpot could not take a large place in a town or anything of that sort, who could tell but the Lord might direct his steps to our little, humble place? And a spirit of prayer and supplication was given me for nearly three years such as I have never before or since experienced for any particular thing, independent of my *own* salvation. I had no rest in my spirit until I had gone up to Stadhampton to see and hear this dear man of God in the church. In the month of October 1833 my wife and I went; we found the church so thronged with hearers that there was hardly standing, much less sitting, room. I had never seen him in my life, but could not fancy the young clergyman standing there in the desk reading the prayers to be he, from the description our dear friend Mr Tiptaft had given of him. At length, after the prayers were read, this young gentleman came down, went to what is called the squire's pew, opened the door, and helped the black gown on to a tall and handsome man, who seemed about thirty years of age. The young curate did it so kindly and affectionately towards our friend that it pleased me much to see it.

'Mr Philpot soon ascended the pulpit, and gave out for his

text 2 Cor. 3 : 15, 16.[1] I stood up all the time, listening to every word that he said, drinking it in like a thirsty ox. Amongst other deep and experimental things, he said that he feared the greater part of his congregation were lovers of pleasure rather than lovers of God, and it was their village feast-day that brought so many to church. The veil of which he had been speaking was over their eyes and hearts, or they could never repeat all those responses they had repeated so loudly, turning and bowing to the east, while some of them were living in the open practice of the very sins they had asked to be delivered from, crying out, "Lord have mercy on us, and incline our hearts to keep this law". Whether it was the squire of the parish, or the meanest pauper, unless they turned to the Lord the veil was not and never would be taken away. I had never heard such faithful preaching in the Church before.

'After the service was over I handed him a note of intro-duction which I had from Mr Tiptaft; he received us very kindly, and at his request we accompanied him across the green to his apartments; and after a little conversation we pre-vailed on him to return with us in our covered conveyance to Abingdon, about eight miles distant. The old landlady, in whose farm-house Mr Philpot had rooms, seemed quite aston-ished that he should think of going out after church-time, in the month of October, and in the evening too; it was a thing she had never known him to do before. On the same evening we all went to Mr Tiptaft's chapel to hear him preach, and a very encouraging, blessed time we had.

'After service I believe we all sat and wept together in Mr Tiptaft's little room. Our two now dear departed friends appeared to be real brothers. We sat up to a late hour, while

[1] 'But even unto this day when Moses is read, the vail is upon their heart. Nevertheless, when it shall turn to the Lord, the vail shall be taken away.'

Mr Philpot talked very freely of his troubles about continuing in the Church, saying that if he had more grace he should not do so, and it was the want of grace and faith that kept him in it. I remember his quoting from Jeremiah, "He hath hedged me about that I cannot get out; He hath made my chain heavy". "The Lord", he continued, "has made me useful and acceptable to many at Stadham and in the neighbourhood, and how can I quit them without some very clear intimation and direction from Him? I know I cannot go back again into the world; but I cannot say I delight myself in the Lord. What a poor minister should I be to a people who have heard and known the truth for years! Saddle myself on such I dare not. Oh that I had wings like a dove! for then would I fly away, and be at rest. Nothing short of an answer that the Lord will be my guide, so that I might see the pillar of cloud going before me, will ever induce me to leave my present post. I should only be a darkener of the Lord's counsel by words without knowledge; for a man may be called by grace without ever being called to the work of the ministry."'

We shall hear more of Joseph Parry in the sequel. Many of my father's letters are addressed to him. His answers, unfortunately, have not been preserved, for though he often said he would sooner ride fifty miles than write a letter, he could evidently compose a touching one when he tried.

Month followed month, and still my father continued irresolute. 'I would sooner be turned out than go out', he writes to his new friend. 'Let them thrust me out of the land of Egypt and the house of bondage, and my way is clear enough. No one knows what it is to give up a people who love you and a situation where the Lord has blessed you, but those who have the trial.' During all those eighteen months which followed his visit to Stadham, Joseph Parry at Allington still went on wrestling in prayer for the thing on which he had set his simple heart. 'My thoughts at that time', he afterwards confessed, 'were more about you than all my business and everything else put together. I remember how, when I used to walk about the orchard, my thoughts used to be running about making preparations for you, if you should come, contriving sometimes one plan and then another. Sometimes, I thought, if you would never come here, I would move to wherever you settled. Still I could never move back from calling upon the Lord that you might come here, though often questioning whether I was right. Nor was I ever easy till, after my begging and entreating, He made a way open and answered my cry. Let whatever will take place, I know there was a real spirit of prayer for you on me then, and I feel satisfied that your coming to Allington was wholly of the Lord.'

How in the end my father found deliverance, not through the pillar and the cloud, not through any 'wonderful leading', but in the still, small voice, must be told in his own words. He is preaching in London on God's method of answering prayer and has pointed out how in many minds there is often a kind of confusion with respect to it.

'They are in a certain path,' he proceeds, 'from which they want to be extricated; they are under a trial, from which they want to be delivered; they call upon the Lord to deliver them; and they ask some manifestation of Himself; some going forth of His hand, some divine leading which they are to follow. But the Lord may be working in a very different way from what they think; and they may really be inattentive to the internal voice of God in their conscience, because they are expecting the voice to come in some other way. It was just so with myself. When I was in the Establishment, burdened with all the things I had to go through, and troubled and distressed in my mind, I was calling upon the Lord to deliver me, to lead me out, to show me what to do, to make the path plain and clear.

Now that was my sincere cry; but I expected some miraculous interposition — to hear some voice, to have some wonderful leading; and in waiting for that, I was waiting for what the Lord never meant to bestow. And I was brought at last to this internal conviction; suppose I were living in drunkenness, suppose I were living in adultery, suppose I were walking in known sin, should I want a voice from God to say to me, "Leave this drunkenness, come out from this adultery, give up this sin"? Should I want some divine manifestation to bring me out of a sin, when my conscience bore its solemn witness, and I was miserable under the weight and burden of it? No; the very conviction is the answer of God to the prayer; the very burden which the Lord lays on us is meant to press us out of that in which we are walking. So I reasoned with myself: "If I am living in sin, if it be a sin to be where I am, if I must do things which my conscience tells me are sins, and by which my conscience is burdened as sins, the very conviction, the very distress, the very burden, is the answer. It is the voice of God in the conscience, not the voice of God in the air, not the appearance of God in the sky, but the voice of God in the conscience, and the appearance of the frown of God in the heart." And on this simple conviction I was enabled to act, and never to this day have repented it. I have, therefore, been led to see by experience, that we are often expecting wonderful answers, mysterious answers, and the Lord does not mean to give those answers.'[1]

The end came at last in March 1835. 'I told only two persons of my intention,' he writes, 'and having on Sunday, 22nd, preached in my usual way, I added at the end, "You have heard my voice within these walls for the last time. I intend to resign the curacy and withdraw from the ministry of the Church of England." It was as if a thunderbolt had dropped in the con-

[1] *Early Sermons,* Vol. I (London, 1906), p. 264.

gregation. I did not wish any excitement, or manifestation of feeling, and therefore shut it up as quickly as possible. The people were much moved and the next day some met me and said that they could build me a chapel, if I would consent to stay. To this, however, I do not feel inclined, though the people wish it much and say it should not cost me a farthing.' In the event, as we shall see, his old hearers did build a chapel, and find a minister after their own hearts to preach in it.

No sooner had Joseph Parry heard that there was at last a prospect of his prayers being answered, than he saddled a horse and rode the thirty or forty miles across the downs to Stadham, to find that my father was with William Tiptaft at Abingdon. He followed him there and wrung from him a promise that he would come and stay with him at Allington and preach in the little chapel as soon as he was free. But first his Fellowship must be resigned and reasons shown. This gave my father the opportunity of issuing, as it were, a manifesto in the form of a Letter to the Provost of Worcester College, which was widely circulated at the time and has since passed through many editions.[1]

There was nothing now to keep him at Stadhampton except the disposal of his books, of which he had a large and valuable collection, including a *Thesaurus* of Stephanus, which had cost him eighteen guineas, and many valuable school and college prizes. These were packed up and sent to London, where their

[1] See Appendix. This letter represents the 'crossing of the Rubicon' by its writer. At this point in his life—its true watershed—he makes his deliberate choice, turns his back once and for all upon the Church of England—his Egypt—and its bondage, and goes out into the wilderness 'leaning upon his Beloved'. He never looks back with longing to the delicacies of the land he had forsaken, but sustained by the 'hidden manna' he follows hard in the footsteps of his Master until finally he 'sees the Canaan that he loved, with unbeclouded eyes'. The letter, though some will consider it couched in extreme terms, deserves very careful reading.

sale occupied three days. Of secular literature he retained only a Milton's *Paradise Lost*, a pocket Dante, and the three slim volumes of Cowper, which had been given to him by his Irish love, and which have happily come down to me.

And then, to quote his own words, 'like Abraham he went forth, not knowing whither he went, but esteeming with Moses the reproach of Christ greater riches than the treasures of Egypt, and little foreseeing either what the Lord in His providence would do for him, or in His grace do by him'. He had no private income, no prospects. Almost every channel of employment was closed to him, and his health was, to say the least, precarious. He obeyed the Gospel injunction, 'Leave all and follow Me', to the very letter. And if he scattered some bitter words in doing it, they may perhaps be forgiven him.

10: Allington and Joseph Parry

'WATER-MEADOWS AT THE BOTTOM, CORNLAND GOING up towards the hills, those hills being *downland*, and a farm-house in a clump of trees, sheltered on every side but the south.' Such roughly was Allington — to borrow the description of his ideal home in a Wiltshire vale by no less an authority than William Cobbett, of the *Rural Rides*. But to me, as a little boy in petticoats, when Florence Nightingale was the idol of the day, Allington was far, far more than that. It was a magic land flowing with milk and honey and loving-kindness, where for a whole month my parents, and especially my gentle mother, were manifestly happy and wonderfully at home. There, too, was the unpretending little chapel by the wayside, hiding its homely face behind its leafy strip of grave-yard, with Joseph Parry, as modest and unassuming, for its chief deacon and supporter. The bluff, weather-beaten farmer with the warm heart and the tender conscience partly owned and wholly ruled the little hamlet, looked up to by all but subordinate to none, except to a shadowy landlord, of whom he held some of his sunny sheep-walks, and who now and then drove across half the county in his bright yellow travelling chariot to talk farm-gossip with his tenants. For Allington sits on the very instep of the Downs, tucked away in a sunny fold just where they soar at their steepest out of the unfenced levels of Pewsey Vale. The feel of the Downs is always there, like the feel of the sea at the seaside, and the cool down-winds sweep over it with almost the snap of a Margate breeze. From there, too, at the cost of a breathless climb, you may launch your mortal shallop on to a green solitude, steer where you will, stretch eye-strings and heart-strings to the cracking-point, and listen in an enraptured silence, broken only by the occasional tinkle of a sheep-bell, to the breathing of a thousand hills. In the dim blue distance, fifteen miles away to the north, lies Swindon, at that time the nearest station.

Pausing on the lip of the scarp before you scramble down again, you have Allington at your feet, a small, compact green jewel of elms and orchards, set on the very edge of the wide brown plain, with here and there a whitewashed gable blinking in the sun and sending up a blue incense-spire into the crystalline air. Just beyond the emerald hamlet, threaded to it almost like necklace to pendant, is a sinuous sky-blue line — a length of baby-ribbon, it might be, carelessly dropped on to the carpet — the Kennet-and-Avon canal, hugging the feet of the Downs, as it curls away to Devizes, six miles to the west, to throw itself headlong by some thirty locks into the Avon valley.

Besides the chapel, Allington consisted when I was a child of a dozen or more old thatched and lime-washed cottages, each standing well back from the shady lane behind its flowered apron; of the low polygonal farmhouse with its deep thatched eaves, where Mr Parry first received my father, and whither he retired again in his old age; of the solid box-like Victorian edifice, built for him when he was burnt out of the other, between the rambling farm-steadings and the big orchard, garrisoned against small bare legs, as I remember to my cost, by spiteful geese and turkeys; and of one other low glorified cottage in a secluded garden, aflame to my memory with tulips, where lived Mr Tuckwell, the junior deacon, and whither I was taken most mornings for some make-believe lessons. And to think that it was only the other day, when I took to poring over old records, that I actually realized what deep heart-searchings, what travail of spirit, what hidings and shinings of God's face all that peaceful loveliness could cover!

A short dip of gritty, sun-baked road takes you down from the cool elm-tree shade across the swing bridge over the canal to lush water-meadows and spreading hedgerows, with wild roses, birds' nests, butterflies, and I know not what other enchantments of a child's paradise. Left to themselves until the hay is in, these fields become at sheep-washing a scene of bucolic bustle. To a chorus of Doric chaff the brown-armed sheep-washers lower themselves to their midriffs into wooden bins, which are sunk in the dry channel almost level with the surrounding meadow. The sluices being drawn, in rushes the brown canal water, and swirls around them. Then with bleatings and shoutings and thwackings innumerable, accentuated by the staccato barks of tense-eared sheep-dogs, the reluctant wool-bearers, fresh from the liberty of the Downs, are forced to take to the water, two or three at a time, and each is poled with a clothes-prop to its appointed place. Hour by hour the busy laundering goes on, until hundreds have received immersion, have left their sinful ticks in the cleansing stream, and have clambered clumsily ashore, to shiver and drip on to the trampled daisies.

Sometimes on still evenings, shadowed persistently by a quivering haze of midges, we saunter along the level tow-path — one of my father's chosen solitudes before a sermon — and watch the painted barges dawdle past, their occupants apparently taking their ease as if life were one long clay-pipe holiday. New-daubed with lemon-yellow, scarlet, white and a hard sky-blue, they seem to a child's eye to partake of the same romantic lineage as the heraldic chariot of Mr Parry's noble landlord.

Except for those stealthy wayfarers, the barges, and for a chance tramp or tourist on his way over the Downs, Allington knows no through traffic. It lies at the end of all things, at the very bottom of the pocket. Scarcely a murmur seems to come from the outer world to trouble the peace that has nested there for centuries. It was not always so. A few fields off, at a couple of spits deep, you may dig up by the score spindle-whorls, fibulæ, hammerstones, pot-sherds, and fragments of crucibles dating back to the iron-workers of the Hallstadt age, who thronged the place before the Romans came. A Sabbath-day's journey distant lie Silbury Hill and all that is left of the big temple of Avebury. But the noisy iron-smelters have long since disappeared. Gone, too, are the white-robed Druids, leaving no successors; not even so much as a resident minister. For the little chapel has to be content with such itinerant preachers as Mr Parry can persuade to come that way. When no such preacher can be procured, a handful of the faithful assemble on the Lord's Day in the big table-pew to pray and sing, as best they can, and to hear a deacon read the Word of truth, followed by the printed sermon of some godly minister.

*

Summer after summer, from 1835 until 1869, the year of his death, all through the hungry forties and the halcyon Victorian days, my father went to Allington for a month before or after the hay harvest, and took his wife and the reigning baby, so long as there was one, with him. How vividly I recall those happy migrations! my father standing on the low Stamford railway platform, in tall silk hat and long cloak, patient and dignified, withdrawn into himself; my beautiful mother flushed and a little 'cumbered' like Martha, till she has us safe on board, yet always with an alert blue eye for any oddity in the crowd. Then long hours on the old broad-gauge, in a half-compartment almost as inviolable as a private post-chaise, with a party-door which a restless imp could latch and unlatch to his heart's content until bidden to desist. Poor as he was, it never occurred to my father that gentle people could travel other than first, with a half-crown for the guard, who handed down our luggage from our own carriage roof. So I remember delicious sleepings and wakings, curled up on the wide drab-cloth cushions, and feastings out of little surprise packets, or on 'Banbury cakes', the very cry of which will thrill me to this day, while my mother, radiantly happy – for is she not speeding away from sneers to smiles, to holiday plenty from incessant pinch? – sings to me, or makes up little jingling rigmaroles, which bring a wintry smile even to her husband's meditative eyes.

Then, the long weary drive from Swindon, under the hood of the phaeton, smelling of the harness-room, behind the fat carriage-horses, and the Dickensian welcome on the doorstep from Mr and Mrs Parry and the two grown daughters, who, to relieve my mother, take immediate possession of me, to wash and brush and put me to bed by turns. Then, to wake up to a sunny morning and the jubilant farmyard cackle! What a lump of emotion is the common barn-door fowl! Then, to canter through the crisp morning air over the trackless downs, perched up before Mr Parry on his saddle-bow! Or hanging on desperately to his kind, rough hand, to watch the four huge yoke-oxen come in from the plough, breathing hard and steering straight for the water trough, like fishing-boats to harbour. Or, after waiting for the crimson embers to be raked out from the big bread oven, and for the batch of cream-faced globes of dough to be ladled in, to feel myself lifted up in stalwart arms and gingerly to push in a baby loaf, all for my own consuming, before the iron door clangs to.

*

When I myself first knew Allington, the pride of twenty summers had passed over it, and my father had so firmly established himself in the confidence of his thousands of hearers and readers, that Envy had begun to carp and mutter 'Pope'. But when he first set foot in Wiltshire in the early summer of 1835, with only Joseph Parry and William Tiptaft for his sponsors, it was as a new and untried man, whom his very birth and education, to say nothing of fine linen and Oxford manner, were calculated to render all the more suspect to the old-established ministers and congregations — for they could hardly as yet be called a sect — with whom he was inclined to throw in his lot. So that, altogether apart from his natural hesitation at quartering himself indefinitely on the Parrys and perhaps of having to take to his bed in the 'prophet's chamber', as in the event he did, he was troubled by doubts and fears as to how far his message would find acceptance. As regards his host, except on the crucial question of baptism, he need have had no misgivings. But his prospective hearers, the Wiltshire farm-hands and peasants, were an unknown quantity. 'As you yourself have often remarked,' we find him writing to Joseph Parry[1] at a later date, 'I need a little time before people can receive my ministry, or enter into my drift. Half a dozen sermons are not

---

[1] Joseph Parry was nearly two years older than my father, having been born at Allington, 23 February 1801, presumably in the old farmhouse at that time in the occupation of his father. He and his wife had married comparatively young, and there were four children in the nursery when my father first stayed with them in 1835. He survived my father by a little more than two years, his widow dying six months later, and they were buried in the same grave in the forecourt of the little chapel. There is a very sympathetic *Memoir* of them in the *Gospel Standard* for January 1872 (Vol. XXXVIII, p. 37) from which I extract the following: 'In Joseph Parry's character there was a singular dignity, coupled with great humility. He was one who could be loved, but certainly not one that any person would have felt inclined to take liberties with. His heart was large and generous. Indeed, we may almost use the word princely, not referring to the means, but to the will to be liberal. He was ever ready to forward the Lord's cause, sending ministers about the country to help the causes which stood in need of it. He was a man of excellent judgment in divine things, both as respects men and doctrines. His own religion had passed through fire and water.'

enough to make it evident.' It is considerations such as these which give their poignant interest to the two rather prickly letters which he addressed to his friend before and after his first visit to Allington, as a paragraph taken from the first of them will show:

Abingdon, 3 *June* 1835

'I hope and pray that I may not come amongst you in vain. How far our views and principles may coincide, I know not; but I shall, God enabling me, faithfully declare what I feel and believe to be true without fearing man. I am on the dark side of things, and more for confusion, guilt, and bondage than liberty, assurance, and freedom. Not that I object to the *realities* of these latter, but to their *counterfeits* so universally current. Neither do I wish to preach to a people who will not or cannot receive me and my doctrine. I come, therefore, to you, as a friend, for a few days, or a few Sundays, just as I and the church suit one another. If I do not suit them, I should be glad to leave Allington after the first Lord's day. If they can hear me comfortably and profitably, I would not mind staying three or four. But I wish it to be understood that I come to see you as a personal friend, and only to preach as a friend staying with you—as a wayfaring man that tarrieth for a night. Expect but little from me and you will be less disappointed, as I am a very poor creature in body and soul.'

As it turned out, instead of staying over only one Lord's day at Allington, my father ended by staying five, and actually promised to return in September for a visit of indefinite duration, after the strenuous days of the harvest were over. By this time his younger sister was already a mother, and on her husband, Capt. S. Ross Watts, being appointed to the guard-ship at Plymouth, H.M.S. *Royal Adelaide*, my impulsive grandmother had left her quiet berth at Walmer and with her elder daughter and invalid son had set up house at Stoke, Devonport, which henceforth became her home. And it was thither that my father went for a brief rest, and to prepare himself for one of the gravest decisions of his life.

Should he be baptized, or not? Should he, or should he not, submit himself to what, short of a martyr's death, is perhaps the severest test that can be applied to the sincerity of a man's Christianity? On the one hand, we find him writing to his friends at Stadham : 'All forms, opinions, rites, ceremonies and notions to me are nothing, and worse than nothing; they are the husks which the swine eat, not the food of the living soul. To have the heart deeply penetrated with the fear of Jehovah, to be melted and filled with a sweet sense of dying love and atoning blood, to have the affections warmed and drawn forth under the anointings of the Eternal Comforter, this is the only religion that can suit and satisfy a regenerate soul.' Moreover, the man he most revered amongst the dead, William Huntington, as well as many other true followers of Christ, living and dead, had not been Baptists. On the other hand, if he could make up his mind to submit, it would best suit his own comfort and convenience. It was the path of least resistance, and therefore the most to be distrusted. The little chapel at Allington was pledged to baptism by its trust-deeds and it was not to be expected that its rustic congregation would consent to sit indefinitely under an unbaptized minister. If the thing on which Joseph Parry had long since set his heart was to find fulfilment, if my father was to make Allington his permanent home, he must be baptized, or else be thrown on the world again. No wonder he was driven this way and that, a prey to conflicting motives.

'You speak of the baptizing', he writes to Joseph Parry on the eve of his return. 'But I have many doubts and fears respecting it. First, I feel my miserable unbelief, sinfulness, hardness of heart, backslidings, ignorance of Christ and manifold corrup-

[117]

tions as most powerful obstacles in the way. Secondly, my poor, weak, shattered, tottering, cold-catching body fills me with many apprehensions. But I trust if I saw Jesus one side the water I should venture through. I seem now to have missed the most favourable opportunity during the warm weather we have just had. But I would add that, if I am to go through the ordinance this year, it must not be pushed into the autumn. 13 September is the last Sunday I could submit to it, and I do assure you I shall be very thankful to escape with a cold. I asked Mr Warburton to baptize me, if I should go through the ordinance, and should not wish any other. If then he is able to come to Allington on 13 September, I would, the blessed Lord enabling me, follow the example of the great Head of the Church, in passing through the waters of Jordan.'

It will be noticed that he is careful to speak of the rite as an 'ordinance' and not as a 'sacrament'. Indeed throughout his life he maintained that Baptism and the Lord's Supper were not sacraments at all, as the Churches of Rome and of England, though not that of Scotland, consider them, i.e. immediate channels of divine grace, but *ordinances*, celebrations or memorials of our Lord's sacrifice, death, burial and resurrection, 'which may or may not be attended with a divine blessing, but are not channels of spiritual life'.[1]

'You ask how I was convinced of believer's baptism', he writes (9 January 1840) to a young brother-minister who was exercised on the point. 'When the subject first arrested my mind, I turned from it with enmity, as I saw it was like a man coming to cut down my apple-tree, which bore the golden apples. This was evident, that if believer's baptism was the only scriptural one, I must relinquish my connection with a system that was based on infant sprinkling. But this I had neither inclination, nor faith to do, especially as my health was in-

---

[1] *Gospel Standard*, January 1867, Vol. XXXIII, p. 22.

different and all my income derived from the Establishment. Still, however, as I read the Scriptures, I could see neither precept, nor example of any other baptism, and together worked with this the awful mockery of the Church of England's service for sprinkling infants, which, however, I escaped, as having an assistant who did that as well as all other formal work. Some friends of mine, too, at this time seceded from the Establishment and were baptized, and as I still maintained equally friendly relations with them, we sometimes conversed upon it, and my convictions were still more strengthened, till they outgrew and outweighed all bonds and shackles, and forced me out of Babylon. I was baptized six months after I left the Establishment and have never swerved from believing it to be a Gospel Ordinance, though I feel little disposed to make a shibboleth of it, or make it a prominent topic of my ministry. The way in which many Baptists bring it forward I much object to, as though it were the all-in-all and the grand turning point, whereas I rather regard it as an Ordinance to be obeyed from divine teaching and love. "If ye love Me, keep My commandments." But some of my dearest friends and best hearers are not Baptists, nor has this come in as a bar, or a stumbling-block between our friendship and love. I cannot, however, agree to make it an indifferent thing, and in our zeal for spiritual substances, to set aside the Lord's clear command, and the apostles' undoubted practice, as nullities and shadows. Jesus is a lawgiver to His chosen and they honour Him little who despise His precepts.'[1]

Scarcely more than a year after he had himself been baptized he writes to Joseph Parry: 'Let us not have separated from ungodly systems and dead professors on account of doctrines only and outward ordinances, however true and scriptural: neither let these things, especially the latter, break the union

[1] *Memoir and Letters of J. C. Philpot* (London, 1871), p. 146.

between the family of God. I am a decided Baptist, but I can stretch my hand across the water to God's children whose eyes are not open to see the ordinance, whilst there are thousands of Baptists to whom I would not willingly hand a chair.'

Later, in a defence of 'strict communion', he wrote: 'I know from experience that baptism is a very heavy cross, and I can honestly say that I felt it a much keener trial to be baptized, than to leave the Establishment. I was tempted in soul and body, in the first to think I was a hypocrite and, in the second, to believe I should have an inflammation of the lungs, or a pleurisy, and so die. I know very well I would have shunned the cross, if I dared.'[1]

But he did not dare, and on 13 September 1835, his thirty-third birthday, he was baptized in Allington chapel by the old Lancashire weaver, John Warburton. 'About a week back', he tells his friends at Stadham, 'I was privileged to follow the dear Lord through the waters of Baptism and never more sensibly felt my unworthiness than on that day. He was pleased to keep me from taking the least cold, to give me more confidence to step into His watery grave than I could have expected from my many bodily and spiritual temptations and exercises. Mr Warburton preached and baptized me with the greatest solemnity, unction and affection.'

William Tiptaft's instinctive attitude to baptism is still more significant. I can find no allusion to it in all his copious letters of this period, nor does he ever speak of his own baptism,[2] or give a hint that his new chapel at Abingdon was being furnished with a baptistery, though I presume that it must have

---

[1] *Gospel Standard*, May 1840, Vol. VI, p. 101. *Strict Communion Vindicated* (London, 1920), p. 10.
[2] The Minute-book of the old Baptist Chapel at Devizes, Wiltshire, records that: 'On Lord's day, 17 June 1832, Mr William Tiptaft, a clergyman of the Church of England, was baptized in the Chapel by Mr Hitchcock.

been. He mentions casually that Mr Husband, the ex-vicar of a neighbouring parish whose secession preceded his own, had licensed his house for divine worship, and was baptizing in a mill-dam close to his old church, an old lady of eighty being amongst the baptized. In July 1834 he writes: 'I spoke to a large multitude assembled together to see Husband baptize four members. I was enabled to speak plainly on the occasion.' And he adds: 'We still talk about baptizing and forming a church here (at Abingdon), but there are so few that I can fully receive in heart and I feel myself so unfit for a pastor. . . . There is nothing worth living for in this vain world. Vanity is stamped upon all created good, and my desire is to die to the world and to be alive unto God.' The great question for him is 'Are we in the right way? Is life communicated to our souls? What is all our preaching, reading, praying and professing, if we have not the root of the matter in us?' No mention either of Baptism, or of the Lord's Supper! Year followed year and they were still talking of the matter.

It was not indeed until January 1843, more than eleven years after he had left the Church, that William Tiptaft was finally able to overcome his scruples, and before a 'very large concourse of people both times', to baptize seven women and five men after the morning service, and six women and five men in the afternoon. 'What a different feeling I had in going down from the pulpit to baptize', he writes, 'from what I used to experience when I had to descend from the pulpit in the Church of England to sprinkle infants, and to give a flat contradiction to what I stated in the pulpit respecting regeneration, etc., at the same time encouraging the blind and ignorant godfathers and godmothers in their sin and mocking of God, who came forward so boldly and carelessly to make such awful vows and promises. I am satisfied that many things may be bought too dear, even gold; but one thing cannot, which is a good conscience.'

To return to my father: 'When first he came amongst us,' wrote Joseph Parry, 'he was very close and searching in his preaching, and it was enough to make a living man tremble. . . . Some, when returning home, would sit down on the roadside and say, "Well, we can never stand this searching preaching, it cuts us up root and branch".' Amongst those who felt themselves thus 'searched', and were inclined to resent it, was actually the junior deacon, Joshua Carby Tuckwell, who shared with Joseph Parry the onus of maintaining the little 'cause'. The son of a naval officer who, after playing a conspicuous part in Lord Rodney's great victory off Guadeloupe (12 April 1782), had left the service and taken a farm in Wiltshire, Mr Tuckwell, as I remember him, was a spare little figure, very neat and precise, whom I always associate with tulips as red as his face, and with 'pot-hooks and hangers', for was it not he, dear man! who first taught me to hold a pen? By that time he had become one of my father's staunchest allies, but it was only after much heart-searching, and if the little deacon had not been of a most gentle and forgiving spirit, I doubt whether the fiery young evangelist would ever again have shown his face in Allington pulpit.

Writing more than thirty-two years later, after he had laid his old friend to rest in the little graveyard on the very eve of his own sixty-fifth birthday, my father admits that owing to his own deep exercises of spirit, his ministry when he first went to Allington was of a very separating and searching character, 'and having much zeal and warmth, as most young soldiers have, I used to cut away right and left, without fearing foe or sparing friend, if I thought him wrong. In this spirit and with this ministry, I went to Allington, where I found a people both there and in the neighbourhood, who had been accustomed to smoother tidings than those which I brought, and as I thought sunk into a dead and flat state of soul. This put a fresh edge on

my sword, and I dare say I cut pretty sharply at a lifeless profession. . . . Some fell under it, others fought against it, and
some did not know what to make of it, partly because it was
a sound to which they were unaccustomed, and partly because
they misunderstood my meaning and drift. Amongst these
latter at that time was Carby Tuckwell. He treated me with
the greatest kindness and respect; but as I sometimes spoke
pretty freely of the state of things at Allington, declaring from
the pulpit that I believed the deacons were in some measure to
blame for it, he was induced to think that I set myself almost
personally against him, that I suspected his religion, and tried
to uproot it, as not being genuine. This was not the case, but
still such was the impression on his mind. He, however,
cordially joined in inviting me to come again; and as my
ministry became better understood and more fully received by
the people, I continued with them not only all the winter, but
remained with them until the autumn of 1836, though I
always declined their repeated wish to be settled over
them.

'During my second visit to Allington (in 1835) I preached
from John 17:3: "And this is life eternal, that they might know
Thee, the only true God, and Jesus Christ, whom Thou hast
sent"; and after pointing out what it was to know the only true
God, by some discovery of His Being, majesty and greatness to
the soul, I went on to show what it was to know Jesus Christ in
the light and by the power of His blessed manifestations. This
sermon fell with great weight and power on Carby Tuckwell's
mind and showed him that my ministry was not directed, as he
thought, against himself or against real religion, but was a
cutting down of what was merely natural and notional in order
to trace out and bring out more clearly the real work of God
upon the soul. . . . This gave him, therefore, a union with me
and my ministry from that time forward. Scores, I might say

[123]

hundreds, of miles have we travelled together in those days when I used to preach at the various little chapels round Allington, as he was always my companion in the vehicle which took me out and brought me back, often quite at a late hour of the night. Nor have I ever had a kinder, more attentive, or affectionate companion and friend.'[1]

To complete the picture, I will include a touching little vignette which my father has left of another old hearer, who was at first terribly depressed by his preaching, but who, nevertheless, would always walk his six miles there to hear him.

'Everyone called him Farmer Wild, and he was a plain, simple English farmer of the old school, honest, straightforward, sober and very industrious. He with his wife had long been chapel-people, but had for some time been sunk into a cold, lethargic and sleepy state of soul. When, therefore, the good farmer was first brought under a more searching, separating ministry than he had been accustomed to, it was very cutting to his feelings, and seemed at times to strip him of all his religion. But, as Mr Huntington somewhere says, "Where we get our cutting, there we get our healing", and thus, as every now and then there was a little balm dropped upon the sore, it nailed his ears fast to the door-post; and I may say almost literally as well as spiritually so, for he always sat close to the door of the chapel, in one and the same place, and I seem to see him now in my mind's eye, for he was naturally one of the finest grown men that I have ever seen, hanging upon the word, as though he could eat it. When the service was over, he would creep away by himself and get under a hedge, or sit on a bank (for hedges are rare things in that part of Wilts), where he ate his dinner alone, rarely speaking to anyone and carrying as he best could his own burden, or feasting on any little morsel

[1] *Gospel Standard,* April 1868, p. 121.

that he might have gathered up under the word.'[1] Farmer Wild, I may add, lived only a couple of years to taste the bitter-sweet of the new ministry.

Although, as will have been seen, my father attached supreme importance to a knowledge of Christ 'in the light and by the power of His blessed manifestations', he was himself, unlike William Tiptaft, extremely reticent in recording his own experience, and the following is the only explicit account I have been able to trace. One morning in November 1844, after he had been confined to bed for three weeks, he was thus blessed. 'I saw nothing', he writes, 'by the bodily eye, but it was as if I could see the blessed Lord by the eye of faith just over the foot of my bed; and I saw in the vision of faith three things in Him which filled me with admiration and adoration. 1, His eternal Godhead; 2, His pure and holy Manhood, and 3, His glorious Person as God-Man. What I felt at the sight I leave those to judge who have ever had a view by faith of the Lord of life and glory, and they will know best what holy desires and tender love flowed forth, and how I begged of Him to come and take full possession of my heart. It did not last very long, but it left a blessed influence upon my soul; and if ever I felt that sweet spirituality of mind which is life and peace, it was as the fruit of that view by faith of the glorious Person of Christ, and as the effect of that manifestation. Happy are they who can say by a sweet revelation of Him to their soul, "And we know that the Son of God is come, and hath given us an understanding, that we may know Him that is true; and we are in Him that is true, even in His Son Jesus Christ. This is the true God, and eternal life" (1 John 5 : 20).'[2]

Such then was Allington, its people, and the ministry of the Gospel there! So long as Joseph Parry lived and reigned, its

---

[1] *Gospel Standard*, April 1869, p. 130.

[2] *Eternal Sonship of the Lord Jesus Christ* (1926). Preface, p. 11.

heart-searching piety and generous farmhouse fare kept pace together. It was a puritan Little Gidding, a pocket Geneva, where uncompromising Calvinism could be studied in pure culture, as little contaminated as possible by the infectious germs of worldliness and self-seeking, or by the pomps and vanities of the order of things from which my father had made his never-to-be-regretted separation.

11: Oakham and Stamford

WE HAVE NOW TO RETRACE OUR STEPS A LITTLE AND
to accompany William Tiptaft, while still vicar of Sutton
Courtney, to his native Midlands, and to two quiet old market-
towns a dozen miles apart, Oakham and Stamford, in each of
which he had a married sister living, tall, handsome, prolific
women to whom he was attached by every fibre of his celibate
heart. Deborah Keal of Oakham was by this time near the end
of her child-bearing, the advent of her eighth and last infant
being awaited. But Eliza Cheselden Phillips, the playmate of
his childhood, and now the wife of a worthy and prosperous
brewer of Stamford, was still in the midst of hers, but by that
time she had already ceased to play any part in her brother's
intimate life. For though he never ceased to love her, nor she
him, yet after she had heard him harangue a motley crowd in
Stamford Assembly Rooms she said curtly, 'William is mad',
and returned to her crowded nursery, and to the child-bearing
which was to hasten her end. Eleven little Phillipses she brought
into the world in less than twenty-five years of married life,
then died worn out, as her mother had done before her, at the
age of forty-seven. And in the fine old church of Saint Martin,
Stamford Baron, where under his ornate canopy lies in effigy
the great Lord Burghley, her sorrowing husband put up to her
memory a costly painted window in the taste of the day. And if
he did not at the same time send a handsome donation to the
poor at Braunston, who had known and loved her as a girl, it
was not William Tiptaft's fault, for I have seen the letters in
which he urged it, adding, however, the characteristic proviso,
that 'it is always safer to take advice than to give it'. In both

letters he sends his love to his eleven motherless nephews and nieces, naming them all in the precise order in which they had come into the world, a testimony both to his wonderful memory and to the strength of his domestic affections.

It was in mid-September 1830, eighteen years, that is to say, before his younger sister's death, that William Tiptaft first journeyed down to Oakham, full of new-born zeal, to preach the everlasting Gospel to all who would deign to hear it. 'I should say from what I myself know,' writes my father, 'and from what I have since heard of him about this period, that this was a signal time for the Lord's blessing to rest on his ministry. No doubt there was much excitement, which came to nothing, much false fire, which soon died to ashes, in the crowds of people who flocked to hear him at the various places where he preached. And yet, as some are still alive (1867) to testify, and others have borne witness on their beds of death, many dead in sin were quickened at this period under his ministry into divine life. His occasional visits to Oakham, where he preached in a large building called the "Riding School", as having been constructed for that purpose by Sir Gerard Noel at the time of our war with France, were signally blessed, and were, indeed, the means of raising up a cause of truth in that town, through the instrumentality of a Mr Keal, who, with his wife, was constrained by the power of the Word to leave about this time the Church of England, and cast their lot in with the despised family of God. His ministry at this period was of a peculiar nature, and very striking both in itself and in its effects. It was chiefly to pull down the strongholds of formality and self-righteousness, to show that there was a divine reality in the religion which God wrought by His Spirit and grace in the heart, and that this religion, if genuine, would be manifested by its effects, in separation from the world and living to the praise and glory of God.'

[128]

On the way home from this first evangelical visit to Oakham, William Tiptaft made the acquaintance at Stamford of a certain Mr de Merveilleux,[1] of Huguenot descent, who had a large medical practice in that town and neighbourhood, and was then a member of the old Independent chapel in Star Lane. 'I believe him to be a lover of gospel truth,' he writes to William Keal, 'and I hope that you will call upon him when you go to Stamford. I met a few friends at his house, and spoke a few words to them. They seemed desirous to hear, and, I trust, are spiritually hungering after the bread of life.'

The result of this new friendship was, that when the young vicar of Sutton Courtney returned to the Midlands in October 1831, soon after his west-country tour, Mr de Merveilleux arranged for him to deliver a public address in the Stamford Assembly Rooms, an interesting group of buildings dating from the days when that ancient borough still had a winter season of its own, and there was the annual bull-baiting, and cock-fights in Lord Exeter's new 'pit' near the George Inn, and ladies in hoops and powdered hair went to their balls and routs in sedan chairs, the last survivor of which, by the way, my father sometimes hired in inclement weather to take him to his chapel.

Here, in the large entertainment room, where the County balls are still held, and where in her unawakened youth, I am told, Deborah Keal, having driven over from Oakham with ostrich feathers in her hair and her young husband by her side, would tread the measures of the time as eagerly as any — here it fell to William Tiptaft to preach, as my father tells us, to a very large but miscellaneous audience. 'His name and connection had brought together a very full and mixed congregation; and amongst them some of the clergy, and many of the most respectable persons of the town and neighbourhood.

[1] Pronounced Mervilow.

Nowise, however, daunted by his congregation, many of whom in time past he had personally known, on he went in his usual way, denouncing with no unsparing language the Church of England, the general Dissenters, etc., and preaching just as he would have done had he been standing in a waggon, which he would have much preferred, before a congregation of rural auditors. Some went out, and others who stayed to the end audibly testified their disapprobation. It was, however, as he used to say, his first and last sermon in the Assembly Room, for it could not again be obtained for that purpose.

'To such a large and mixed congregation, deep, experimental preaching was not adapted. This would come afterwards, when they were sifted and separated from the surrounding mass; but for the present a more simple, elementary testimony was needed; for, without having an experience themselves, how could his hearers understand, or enter into a purely experimental ministry? But they could understand, and feel too, at least many of them, his short, sharp knocks against the door of conscience, and his short, pithy sentences, which in a few words cut up, root and branch, all false religion. Not less striking were his bold statements of doctrinal truth, for he did not wrap up election in a few fine phrases which give no offence because they convey no definite meaning, but brought it forward in a way so clear as to lie level with the simplest capacity, and yet so plain and pointed, that the hearers must either rise up in wrath and enmity against it, or fall under it as a Bible truth.'

Amongst the latter in this instance was John George de Merveilleux himself. The effect on him was such that he forthwith severed his connection with the Independents, and decided to build at his own expense a chapel in which the truths, to which his eyes had been, as it were, miraculously opened, might be faithfully and regularly preached. But an unexpected difficulty presented itself. Stamford was then a typical pocket-borough, and the reigning Marquess of Exeter, who was influential in the counsels of the Tory party and already owned more than half the town, snapped up every vacant site almost before it came into the market, to protect his political monopoly; though it is but fair to admit that he selected as his nominees such promising embryo-statesmen as the future Lord Salisbury, and his faithful henchman, Stafford Northcote. Even when with difficulty Mr de Merveilleux had found a site, outside the town-wall and with a somewhat unsavoury approach, he dared not disclose the object of his purchase. Purchased, however, it was, and William Tiptaft had the satisfaction of preaching over its foundation-stone, and of opening it eventually for public worship in 1834. From first to last, site and chapel, after gallery and vestry had been added in 1838, cannot have cost Mr de Merveilleux less than £1,000, a considerable sum in those days, and until his lamented death in 1843, when he was buried within its precincts, he took no rent for it, and bore all the expenses himself, every seat being free.

*

The ancient towns of Stamford and Oakham, which will henceforth play a leading part in our narrative, must have been originally laid out on quite different plans. Stamford, being situated on the Great North Road, arose as a ford-head, a walled parallelogram, guarding the only easy passage across the Welland between the Fens of Lincolnshire on the east and the hills of Rutland on the west. Once over the river, the Scots, Picts and other wild raiders from the north, who in times past were a standing terror to the Stamford burghers, had easy access to the rich pastures of the south, and even to London. Before the Reformation, thanks to the security afforded by its walls, Stamford, as a centre of the wool trade, sheltered many thriving industries, swarmed with monks and nuns, and was within an ace of becoming the seat of a university. It still has six churches, out of an original sixteen, can boast of that anomaly, a dean without a chapter, and to this day retains an unmistakable odour of surpliced sanctity, though it is not less plagued, I fear, with secret sin than any other town of its size. As a little boy, I had often chatted with Corby, the Stamford murderer, who was to all appearance a quite respectable old carpenter, when he came on odd jobs to our house in Rutland Terrace.

In all the six churches, and even in the two chapels, the old red-brick Independent meeting house in Star Lane, and the newer Wesleyan chapel on Barn Hill, the fear of God was still taught, if taught at all, 'by the precept of men', not burnt into the individual conscience through the work of the Holy Spirit. It is true that since the early eighteen-twenties a few poor people had met for private worship at the house of 'honest John Morris', a saddle-tree maker who, when my father first came to Stamford in 1836, welcomed him with open arms.

Oakham, on the other hand, lying as it does in more broken country, cupped in a fertile vale almost engirdled by hills, had less to fear than its neighbour from the fierce northern raiders; while the whole county of Rutland, of which it is the chief town, never harboured more than one small priory, that of Brooke, close to Braunston. Nevertheless, as a glance at its plan will show, Oakham, though an open town, had its own primitive system of defence. No high road passes through it, so that William Tiptaft on his visits had to leave the coach at Uppingham and drive his last six miles in a fly. The approaches to the town itself are still narrow and tortuous. The High Street, fairly wide, is contracted at either end into a bottle-neck, easy to barricade. The Market Place leaves it at a right angle and is partly blocked at its lower end by a row of open stalls known as The Shambles. It then bends to the left and widens into a closed area whose only other exit or entrance is a narrow footway leading to the church and open fields. All has been planned expressly, it would seem, to defend the vital centre of the town in an age when spear-thrusts, sword-cuts, and slings and arrows were all men had to provide against.

Centrally placed near the end of the open space, or *cul-de-sac*, here about a hundred feet wide, is the Butter-cross, a venerable structure consisting of a high-pitched octagonal roof, supported on eight stout wooden pillars, with a stouter one in the centre, rising from three tiers of stone steps. Here on market-day a hundred years ago the pleasant farm-wives used to sit with their week's produce at their feet, butter and eggs, poultry, fruit, mushrooms, and I know not what else, while their husbands displayed their samples of corn, or higgled over their live-stock, on the cobbled space around. For in those days the Butter-cross was the very hub and centre of the town, the lineal descendant, it may be, of its primitive hearth and altar, the symbol of its pristine purpose — peaceful marketing.

Now, when the winter sun mounts above the low houses at the distant end of the Market Place, it casts the peaked shadow of the Butter-cross on to a rambling old stone house, rising to three storeys in the middle, which occupies the whole hundred feet at the top end of the *cul-de-sac* with the exception of its stable-yard entrance to the south and the narrow footway to the church on the north. Here, in this old house, where his father had practised and reared his own brood before him, William Keal lived for close on fifty years with Deborah his wife, and brought up his eight well-favoured children. Here, in his unregenerate days, when they were still a young married couple, William Tiptaft nearly died of typhoid fever. From it he sallied forth to preach the gospel at the Riding School and in the outlying villages; and hither in 1838 he brought his

[133]

broken body to be put together again. Here my mother passed her girlhood and tried to teach her four unruly younger sisters, until my father came and wooed and won and set her free. Here for more than twenty years, from Queen Victoria's coronation until shortly before the death of the Prince Consort, he spent four days in every fortnight and preached at The Factory, a quiet study at the back of the house, which opened on to a little walled garth, being set apart for his sole use. And here as a child I passed most memorable times. With scarce an effort I can look back and see my grandfather on a rainy day trotting up the Market Place, cased in macintosh and spattered with mud from head to foot, changing his grey horse for his roan, and trotting off again on another long round. In memory I can again cross the square carpeted hall, where lived the old grey parrot on its perch, squeeze my small body through the red-baize, brass-studded swing-door, and make my way into the airy, stone-paved kitchen, where my benign old grandma, in fine lace cap and snowy overall, and her three unmarried daughters are seated round a table, all slicing vegetables for the huge copper-full of soup, which is brewing for the poor in the wash-house. I can hang about the busy surgery, where my friend Mr Adcock, the dispenser, is making up my grandfather's prescriptions, rolling pills, deftly spreading plaister or blister, and wrapping up bottles of mixture or liniment with a magic wrist. Or perhaps, with the parrot shrieking after him, 'Adcock, Adcock,' in my grandfather's voice, he will take me up all those stairs to the drug-loft with its barrels, carboys, Winchester quarts and all the surgical stores which a country doctor had to keep on hand when it took days to get a parcel down from London by stage-coach or carrier's cart. Oh! it was a strenuous life that went on in the old house, whether in surgery, stable-yard or kitchen. No stint of food, nor of work!

[134]

One last trivial memory, if only to recall how beneath that busy, cumbered surface there flowed all the while a deep and silent stream. My parents are away and William Tiptaft has come to fill the Oakham pulpit for my father. We are all assembled in the sunny dining room for morning prayers, my grandparents, Uncle Tiptaft, my three comely but as yet unmarried aunts, the country-bred servants, and my small self. After my uncle has read a chapter from the Bible with his beautiful enunciation, we turn our backs upon the laden breakfast table and the singing tea-urn, and fall on our knees at chair or horse-hair sofa. There is an unusual pause. Then from Uncle Tiptaft, 'You pray, William'. 'No, you, William', from my grandfather. 'No, you.' And William Keal proceeds to pour out his heart in broken accents to the Lord of grace. When I think of the formal prayers, indifferently intoned, which I have since had sometimes to listen to, this tender, trivial memory comes back to me like a breath of the morning. God seemed very near that day.

My grandfather was tall and spare, with a narrowish head, a fresh-coloured face, eyes of forget-me-not blue, like my mother's, fine silky hair and a close-cropped, crinkly beard, both silvered when I knew him. He had been an athlete in his youth, and was a man of great physical strength and prodigious energy. Though much of his day would probably be spent in the saddle, he would be up with the lark, digging and trenching in his distant garden to provide vegetables for his hungry family and his wife's soup-kitchen. He had, I believe, an excellent bedside manner, and his patients were devoted to him. Obstinacy was, I think, his foible. His opinion once formed, he stuck to it through thick and thin, and persisted, for instance, in bleeding, blistering and drenching his patients, long after such drastic measures had gone out of fashion. Perhaps in those full-fed, free-drinking days he may not have been wholly

[135]

wrong. He was not a great reader, and seldom opened a book. *The Stamford Mercury*, *Bell's Weekly Messenger*, and the newly-founded *Lancet* told him all that he wanted to know. Until——

Yes, until William Tiptaft insisted on making both him and his wife partakers in his own great discovery—for it is a great discovery, which the present generation, parsons I fear included, seems inclined to fling away—the discovery, I mean, of the Bible as a bosom friend and not a mere bowing acquaintance. 'Read your Bible frequently', he wrote to them. 'Get well acquainted with it.' 'Read Paul's Epistles. They beautifully throw light on the other Scriptures.' And soon, in their rare moments of leisure, the Bible was seldom out of my grandparents' hands. It brought them, I think, nearer together. Indeed, it might be said without much extravagance that, like William Tiptaft and the rector's daughter, they renewed their spiritual courtship over an open Bible. And in the difficulties which lay ahead of them, they would need all the support it could give. 'It must be a source of great joy and delight', wrote his brother-in-law, 'that you and your wife think alike, that you can provoke one another to love and good works, and cheer one another under the persecution of a wicked world.'

As my father wrote in his Preface to William Tiptaft's Letters, 'What he said, he knew; what he wrote, he felt. He never set his foot down to lead others by an untrodden way. He had gone over it night and day, till he thoroughly knew the track, and then he could say with confidence, "Follow me". Those, therefore, who have read his letters with the attention they deserve, will need no telling how urgent and insistent was the spiritual pressure he brought to bear upon my grandfather and his wife. But to what extent he backed it up, when he came to visit them, by word of mouth and fervent prayer, by the example of his self-denying life, and by the fervour of his preaching in the crowded Riding School, must be left to the imagination. We can only judge by the ultimate results, which, briefly, were that my grandfather, his wife, his three maiden sisters, Sarah, Rebecca, and Louisa Keal, broke away from their little world, 'came out from among them', gave up their sittings in the parish church and eventually pooled their resources to convert two floors of a derelict silk factory, which my grandfather had recently purchased, into a Calvinist chapel, where they might sit under a minister known to be sound in the faith. Thereafter for forty years, in the absence of such minister, which happened every fortnight in my father's time, William Keal, until stricken down in the very act of worship, conducted the services himself, read the Bible, followed by some published sermon, engaged in prayer, and led the hymns, for which his musical endowment and tuneful voice eminently fitted him.[1]

Of course, as William Tiptaft had amply warned them, they had much to put up with from their little self-satisfied Oakham world. It was not so much the doctrines they professed, amply covered as they were by the Articles of the Church, as their claim to the right of private judgment, and still more to the right of private feeling, which made their old church-going friends so hot against them. Though the days of overt persecution were happily long past, those who a hundred years ago obeyed the divine command, 'Come out from among them and be ye separate, saith the Lord,' could expect no more consideration from the 'them' than the Lollards received from Archbishop Arundel. So my grandparents became, in William Tiptaft's phrase, 'speckled birds' in their little world. The birds round about were against them (Jer. 12:9), and they had to endure the cruel pecking which is the 'speckled bird's' fate.

[1] For Obituary notice, see *Gospel Standard*, August 1874, Vol. XL, p. 331.

Had they not, I should scarcely be troubling after all these years to write about them. As William Tiptaft was fond of quoting,

The greatest evil we can fear,
Is to possess our portion here.

At one time it looked as if my grandfather might have to give up his comfortable abode and seek his fortunes in a less censorious neighbourhood, so many of his best-paying patients forsook him. But he hung on, and sooner or later they grew tired of spiting their health to nurse their prejudices, and mostly came back, so that by the time I knew him there was scarcely a house in Oakham, or a country-seat in the neighbourhood – and Rutland is full of country seats – where his was not a welcome presence. Finches, Noels, Lowthers, Cecils, Heathcotes – I can well remember the bated breath with which such and other historic names were mentioned across the dinner table, for in those days, you may be surprised to hear, the fear of the Almighty did not necessarily preclude a deep-seated veneration for their little mightinesses, the county magnates.

*

It was in the early summer of 1836 that Sarah Keal, just turned eighteen, with her education completed, came home from her Stamford boarding-school to help in the house and teach her young sisters in place of the much-loved family governess who had now to part from them. The schoolgirl's family album carries us back over a century to the grief of that day when their friend Miss Nettlefold recorded her 'Farewell'; henceforward her presence in the nursery of the busy Market Place house passed into the realm of childhood memories.

Scarcely is the grief of parting over before my father comes down for the first time to Oakham. They have heard much of him from Uncle Tiptaft and are full of expectation. He arrives on 1 July 1836, but, having caught cold on the journey, has to keep his room for some days, and the family do not see much of him. He is able, however, to preach twice on Lord's Day, 10 July, and on the following Wednesday evening. On the Friday, a cold and rainy day, Mr de Merveilleux sends a fly to take him over to Stamford. Sarah Keal having begged him to write something in her album, he has taken it away with him, and does not give it back to her until he is stepping into the fly. This is what she reads, or rather, must ask her brother James to read to her.

> Χαλεπὸν τὸ μὴ φιλῆσαι·
> Χαλεπὸν δέ καὶ φιλῆσαι·
> Χαλεπώτερόν δέ πάντων,
> Ἀποτυγχάνειν φιλοῦντα.

Below he hastily added an improvised translation, for which I have the temerity to substitute my own.

> 'Tis hard to keep from loving; ay!
> And hard with love to burn.
> Hardest of all it is to love,
> And love without return.

This little epigram owes its neatness to a play upon the word 'chalepon', which both in Greek and English may mean 'hard to endure' as well as 'hard to put in practice'.

I doubt whether my father gave his whole mind to it when he inscribed that old Greek school-tag and his hurried translation in the little album. What else could he do when a pretty girl, the daughter of his host, asked a favour of him so prettily. Possibly he would never see her again. For it was not until a fortnight later that he definitely promised my grandfather, whom he found 'a particularly friendly person', to come again to Oakham in the following October. My grandmother also had conceived a warm, almost motherly interest in him. That racking cough of his went to her heart.

Early in October then, my father is back at Oakham, where, as we know, he will remain, except for a month at Stamford, until the spring of 1837 is well advanced. He is by now quite at home in my grandfather's house. Sometimes when the weather is mild he takes a quiet walk with my grandmother, or goes for a ride with her husband, but the family do not see much of him, for he is at his desk nearly all day. But he joins them all at family prayers and at meals. When the mid-day dinner has been served, one of the young ladies knocks at his study door, and in he comes to find all the eight little olive plants seated round the table. At its head sits my grandmother in her fine lace cap, opposite to the curtained windows through which she can look down the long Market Place. He takes his seat on her right hand next to young James Keal. Opposite to him sits Sarah between her two baby brothers, William and John. Eliza, Charlotte, Emma, and pretty little Mary are placed on either side of my grandfather, and sometimes his assistant will come in to complete the round dozen. Having asked a blessing at my grandmother's request, all through the meal my father talks most entertainingly, and the children watch him with wide-open eyes. Before his coming, except during Uncle Tiptaft's visits, meals had been mainly silent.

From this point onward there is to be read between the lines of his letters to Joseph Parry of Allington a moving little intimate drama which lends to them a personal interest. Owing to his invalid childhood, his studious youth, and, later on, his deep absorption in the things of the Spirit, my father had become extremely dependent on the help and service of others. Few men, I venture to say, were ever less fitted to live alone. Fortunately, there were always kind friends at hand,

[140]

who were willing and eager to serve, and, if I may say so, to 'spoil' him. In these letters, if carefully read, will be found hints of two households, each competing for the privilege of aiding him, in gratitude for the spiritual sustenance which he could be the means, under Providence, of conveying to them. One might also go to the length of personifying these two rival habitations. On the one hand, the remote Wiltshire farmhouse, with its uninterrupted leisure and the intimate companionship of his dear disciple, Joseph Parry, than whom no man came ever nearer to his heart. On the other hand, the old house in Oakham Market Place, which I have been at such pains to describe, with its busy coming and going, its anxious, over-driven but deeply religious parents, and its bevy of handsome, high-spirited young daughters, the eldest of whom is already her mother's right hand. There is no mention of her in the letters, but she is there, I might say providentially there, her blonde placidity and even temper the very foil and make-weight to my father's more highly-strung and sombre temperament.

12: The year of attachments

I HAVE BEFORE ME A SHABBY LITTLE TUCK-IN POCKET book, measuring some six inches by four, and bearing on its front fly-leaf the signature and date, 'J. C. Philpot, 1837'. It is my father's Diary for one of the most critical years of his life, and the only one which he preserved, though he took care to run a thick pen through its most self-revealing confessions. It takes us back to a vanished world, to a slow-moving, home-keeping and blessedly noiseless world, except for crowing cocks and church bells and the post-horn and the rare voice of God in the thunder; a world of stagecoaches, gigs, dogcarts and the hired fly, of toil, thrift, hardship and dreadful poverty; a world which on the whole still honoured God with its lips, though its fear towards Him was mostly 'taught by the precept of men' (Isa. 29:13).

In such a world, viewed as it was by him mainly as a fore-court to the Temple of Eternity, secular events hardly counted. In the middle of 1837 old King William died and young Queen Victoria came to the throne, but that epoch-making event is not even mentioned. Yet incidentally we learn much from the Diary which may interest the modern reader. In 1837, for instance, one could get one's hair cut for sixpence, but it cost nearly a shilling to post a letter. Envelopes, postage stamps and 'safety matches' were quite unknown, and every writing table had to be furnished, at least in summer, with tinder-box, tapers and sealing wax. All this and more I know, because my father, who was at that date a poor man, dependent on generous friends for board and lodging and on his preaching for coach fares and pocket money, carefully put down every penny he spent, as well as the few pounds he was able to earn.

It was his last year of freedom, if freedom it could be called; the last full year in which he was not definitely tied to a chapel, or a journal, or a wife. Before it ended we find him pledged to all three. In spite of indifferent health it was a strenuous year, in the course of which he prepared for the press his two best-known sermons: *The Heir of Heaven walking in Darkness and the Heir of Hell walking in Light* and *Winter afore Harvest*.

The Diary is that of a scholar, at home in other languages than his own. The daily note of the weather, on which for him so much depended, and other simple events are recorded in plain English. When kept indoors all day by the weather and his weak chest, the fact is noted in abbreviated French, as *chez moi*, or *au logis t.l.j.* (toute la journée). But avowals of his mental or spiritual state are invariably veiled from prying eyes in Latin. *Ad omnia misere socors* – 'wretchedly careless about everything' – is a not uncommon entry. It means, I think, that for the moment he had exhausted his nervous energies, had emptied his cisterns and must mark time till they refilled.

I must linger over these first few weeks of 1837, even if I have to hurry over the rest, for they saw the early beginnings of what were to be my father's two most providential attachments – his connection with the *Gospel Standard*, and his dawning love for Sarah Keal. Close study of the Diary has convinced me that never did the Lord take better care of him, to borrow his own phrase, than when He bestowed on him the even-tempered helpmate that he needed and the very work he was cut out for. The *Gospel Standard* was at this time over a year old. The first number came forth from an obscure Manchester printing office on 1 August 1835, published by an

[143]

energetic compositor, John Gadsby, the twenty-seven-year-old son of a widely-known and highly-respected minister of the Gospel, William Gadsby. It struggled on for some years short of capital and copy, and John Gadsby was constantly begging my father to contribute to its pages.

The Diary opens on Sunday, 1 January, with a note of the texts he has just preached from at Stamford, where he is staying with Mr de Merveilleux, who lives next door to that very Assembly Room in which he had received his call by grace some six years earlier. A sorely tried man is Mr de Merveilleux. Consumptive like my father, he has a prolific wife, who goes out of her mind and has to be sent away after every confinement. She is away all this month of January. Her only son, a promising child, is fated to die of tubercular meningitis. But his father will die first, before the age of fifty, and will be buried in the vestibule of the chapel he has built at his own cost. And many hundred times, as child and boy, will my unheeding young feet tread over his honoured grave.

On Monday (2 January), 'the cold being very intense', my father stays in all day working hard till close on midnight to finish the MS. of the sermon he had preached in this very town of Stamford only a few weeks back. It is the famous sermon aforementioned, *The Heir of Heaven walking in Darkness*, etc., and few sermons of the nineteenth century are more certain of survival.

Three days later (5 January) he leaves Stamford for the comfortable home of my grandparents, Mr and Mrs Keal, at Oakham, which he had left only a month ago, and which, little as he knows it, is to be his second home for a quarter of a century, the fly taking most of the morning to cover the dozen hilly miles (Tinwell toll-gate, one shilling). The eight high-spirited young Keals, ranging in age from four to eighteen, who are to be his housemates for the next ten weeks, form a striking contrast to Mr de Merveilleux' sickly brood. At Oakham, bodily speaking, my father is in clover. My dear old grandmother, William Tiptaft's sister, delights in spoiling him. He can have breakfast in bed when unwell, and a fire in his bedroom, and also, of course, in the little study set apart for his sole use, quiet enough except for the school-room piano overhead. But he pays for his firing the sum of one pound, I see, which, with canal-borne coal even at eight shillings the ton, should well outlast his projected stay.

6–12 January he spends happily enough in revising his MS. sermon; but no sooner has he got it off his hands than he is again lamenting his wretchedness. For he has fallen, as he often did at this period of his life, into that condition of nerve-fag which the poet Burns has so aptly described as 'restless sloth'. He can settle to nothing. He takes up his MS., *The Two Religions*, destined never to be finished, and puts it down again. He reads this, that and the other, Algebra, Chemistry, Grammar, and helps that promising youth, James Keal, with his Greek until stopped by the influenza which happens to be raging in town and country, but attacks him only mildly. Then, as if providentially, he receives for notice in the *Gospel Standard* a sermon by Mr Nunn, an Evangelical clergyman of Manchester, thought well of by William Gadsby. He works off some of his irritability by 'slating' it unmercifully, and sends off his review by return of post. The next day John Wade of Uppingham brings him a letter he has written, 'To a Friend under Temptation'. My father approves of it, revises it, and gets Sarah Keal to make a fair copy of it. And off it goes, to satisfy John Gadsby's urgent cry for 'copy' (postage on the two letters, one and nine). He need not have hurried, for the letter is held over till March and the Review till April, and is then not printed as an editorial, but as a signed contribution. Truth to tell, the editors are as yet a little afraid of J.C.P. and his terrible outspokenness. For he has not yet learnt to temper valiancy with discretion, nor to speak comfortably to the weaker brethren.

These tasks done, he falls into worse despondency, and on Saturday, 21 January, he tells his Diary, in Latin, that 'being too indolent to settle to anything, I frittered away my time on trifles, most miserably indifferent to all things spiritual or profitable'. And for his morning text on the morrow he chooses, 'I am full of confusion; therefore see Thou mine affliction' (Job 10:15).

He has, indeed, reason enough to feel confused and afflicted. In the first place, all this month of January he is 'suffering from chest and throat', and confined to the house by the bitter weather, except on the four Lord's days, when he has to brave the cold and fulfil his engagements. So he dons his white choker and tall silk hat, and wraps himself up in the cloak with the Astrakhan collar, which he had purchased in wealthier days, and walks through the snow, or is driven in an open dogcart to chapel, morning and afternoon. On one occasion he has to preach in spite of a raging wisdom tooth, which three days later is extracted by my grandfather, not without difficulty. Secondly, my father, by nature a proud, sensitive man, brought up with expensive tastes—this very Diary must have cost him half-a-guinea—finds it galling to have to live on the charity of friends, who may or may not, though providentially they do, find his services worth paying for. Mr de Merveilleux has just given him ten pounds for his month at Stamford, and thirty shillings of it have already gone in charity and tips. At Oakham Mrs Keal will teach him the virtue of thrift, but silently and by example. For of my two grandmothers, Deborah Tiptaft is as thrifty as Maria Lafargue is inclined to be the reverse. Mrs Keal keeps a generous table, but in her house there is no waste, and the poor reap the benefit. With her, charity really does begin at home. Thirdly, my father is being tortured by the thought that in his growing affection for my mother he is being disloyal to the treasured memory of his lost Irish love, of whom he still hears now and again from a mutual friend. He cannot know, as we do, that her death (28 September 1837), following close on that of his invalid elder brother (23 April), will change the whole situation. Lastly, but by no means least, he is in daily terror of being 'altogether left to his foolish and empty self', a perennial source of anxiety to the child of God.

On Monday, 23 January, the proofs of his Sermon arrive and, in spite of his 'confusion' and an aching tooth, he stays up till midnight revising them and writing the Preface, which has unfortunately dropped out of the latest issue. The first edition of 1,500 copies is rapidly sold out, and on 4 March, while still at Oakham, he writes a preface for the second. Before the year is out six editions will have been published, and he will be offering his publisher the stereotype plates. For by then his brother's death will have placed him beyond the need of writing for gain. Indeed, until near the end of his life he will use his pen only for the glory of God and the edification of His people.

By the end of January my father's esteem for Mrs Keal's eldest daughter Sarah (the 'S.K.' of the Diary) was growing rapidly. Frequently was she in and out of his little study, helping him in every way she could. Evidently Mrs Keal was either a very simple or else a very astute mother, as well she might be with five daughters to find husbands for. One day, as the two of them were out walking together they chanced to meet Miss Sarah. 'Here comes my great gawk!'[1] cried my grandmother. 'Oh, don't say that, Mrs Keal', murmured my father in pained protest. His remark sufficed to show her which way the wind was blowing.

---

[1] 'Gawk': An awkward, ungainly person.

It was on 16 February, a Thursday, that matters came to a head. For a whole week, as the scored-out entries tell, my father had been distracted and irresolute, his mind harping on his old Irish love-affair. 11th. 'Thought much of . . . full of it all day; wrote *au soir* (in the afternoon).' 13th. 'slept indifferently'; *au logis t.l.j.* 'unable to apply my mind to anything'. 14th. 'thought much of writing to . . . during night; full of it all morning.' 15th. 'mind full of trouble all day.' 16th. 'slept better; mind less harassed; at intervals troubled; committed matter to the Lord.' Then '*S.K. primum osculatus sum*' (I kissed S.K. for the first time). And found apparently that her heart was his already and that her mother knew it, '*mater haud inscia*'. In the judgment of the world he would no doubt be indiscreet to engage himself to an almost penniless girl, whom he might not be able to marry for years. Who could have then foreseen how providentially obstacle after obstacle would be removed from the path of the lovers?

On Lord's day, 26 February, he preached at Oakham to a very large congregation, including Mr de Merveilleux and John Morris, soon to be deacons of the church at Stamford, and Mr Paulet, who had driven over to invite him to become their settled and salaried minister, and who drank tea at Market Place House before going back to Stamford. Thus was the first obstacle removed!

So happy was my father henceforth at Oakham, as shown by the few erasures in his Diary, that he was easily persuaded to stay an extra week, which meant writing to Mr Creasey at Leicester, to John Kay at Abingdon, and to Joseph Parry at Allington, that they must make other arrangements for filling their pulpits on the days he had arranged to be with them. At length on 15 March he catches at Uppingham the coach for Leicester, and arriving there about six p.m., goes that evening with Morgan, Mr Creasey's deacon, to hear old

Mr Chamberlain. On Thursday, 16 March, he preaches at Mr Creasey's chapel to 'a very large congregation', and receives for it one pound, which is ten shillings short of his next day's coach fare to Oxford. For his ten weeks at Oakham, however, Mr Keal and the friends have given him £30, which he pays into his Oxford bank and raises thereby his small savings to £400. Then after preaching at Abingdon, and spending the inside of a week there, mostly in bed, he reaches Allington, 'snow deep and roads heavy', in time to stand in the familiar pulpit on Lord's day, 26 March.

He has promised to stay at Allington for eight weeks, but four of them are hardly past before the unexpected death at Devonport of his elder brother, poor Augustus, transforms all his worldly prospects and removes one more of the obstacles to his marriage. Under his father's will he comes into the modest patrimony of between three and four hundred a year. No more need henceforth to write for money, nor to jot down every penny he spends! From young John Gadsby, his new employer, he will as yet neither ask nor expect a sou. For the next twenty years he will write only for the love of God and the good of His people.

Meanwhile the news of his engagement has leaked out, and he receives from William Tiptaft, the young lady's uncle, a letter 'kind and wise' but disapproving, by which he feels 'much cut up'. At Allington he finds plenty of leisure not only to finish his pamphlet, 'the great question answered', *What is it that saves a Soul?* but to go carefully through John Warburton's *Memoirs*, the publication of which he strongly recommends. He had counted on meeting him at Calne, but poor old harassed John has to be elsewhere 'about his son Gideon's affairs'.

During the greater part of June my father rests from his labours in his mother's house at Stoke. While there he has his portrait painted, ruins his handwriting for good by taking lessons on an entirely wrong principle, and goes three times to hear 'the poor mason', Arthur Triggs, later on to be connected, not too successfully, with Gower Street chapel.

One 23 June, three days after the accession of Queen Victoria, my father takes coach from Devonport to Exeter, where he preaches that evening from Heb. 4:12.

Saturday 24 June: Unable to sleep for ——s (unmentionable bedfellows); left Ex. at 8 for Bath; went out, 10/-, v. fine and warm. Reached B. 20 p. 6; took fly to Trowbr.; slept at Warburton's.
Sunday 25: Preached at Trowbridge. Mor. Job 18:9. Evg. Isa. 18:5, 6.[1] v. hoarse both times.

No sooner is he back at Allington than he hears that, in spite of the change in his fortunes, there is trouble about his engagement. Mischief-makers have been afoot, scandalized that his choice should not have fallen on some lady of more suitable age. Preposterous! they cry, that a man of thirty-five, and consumptive at that, should think of marrying a beautiful girl not yet nineteen. 'Letter fr. Mrs Keal ab. Miss M. and dear S.L.K.; much exercised; wrote to Mrs K. to give up all present ideas of S and to wait. Much cut up in mind, but felt I had no alternative.'

(To save space I may say here that, though others besides William Tiptaft still disapproved, my grandmother helped my father in every way she could, and, though there were difficulties I may not disclose, had the satisfaction of seeing my parents married in little more than a year from this date, on 24 July 1838.)

During the last days of July 1837 my father rides or drives

[1] The well-known sermon, *Winter afore Harvest.* See letter to Joseph Parry, *The Seceders*, Vol. I, p. 322.

six miles almost daily to comfort Farmer Wild, the hearer aforementioned, on his death-bed, and having had by then to leave Allington for Abingdon, he drives back forty miles across the Downs on purpose to bury him. For he had promised to preach on Lord's day, 30 July, at the opening of the chapel which his former parishioners had built at Stadhampton. Then after fulfilling a fortnight's engagement at 'Zoar' in Great Alie Street, and preaching on a week-evening for Daniel Smart at Welwyn, he takes coach for Uppingham, and, after being driven inside by a thunder-storm, reaches it at 8.15 p.m. 'Took a fly to Oakham; *omnia satis jucunda. S. absens.*' (All things pleasant enough, though Sarah happens to be away.)

On the following Lord's day morning, 20 August, he again preaches the sermon *Winter afore Harvest* and gets into his subject better than at Trowbridge, 'though most probably the printed sermon will differ from both'.

Thursday 24: Drove out w. W.K. (William Keal); walked *au soir* w. Mrs Keal and the ladies, mushrooming.

On the 26th my grandfather drives him in his gig to Greetham on the Great North Road to catch the coach for Nottingham, where he preaches twice on the Lord's day and again on the Tuesday evening.

Tuesday 29 August: at 12 walked to Wilford, dined there and returned in the carriage; preached at Sion Chapel, 1 Cor. 16. 5. good cong.

In later years my father was often entertained as an honoured guest either at Wilford House or at the Bank House, Nottingham, by Mr Henry and Lady Lucy Smith, who had given such friendly support to Thomas Hardy.[1] On the last day of August he leaves Nottingham at 7 a.m. by the Derby mail

---

[1] (1790–1833). The minister of Zion Chapel, Leicester.

through Matlock and Buxton, and at 3.40 p.m. arrives at Manchester, where he is met at the coach office for the first time in the flesh, I believe, by John Gadsby.

Monday 4 September: Letter fr. S.L.K. *pleine d'amour* (full of love). Walked into Manr. Town wretchedly dirty.

In the middle of the week he goes over to Liverpool by 'the new rail-road', walks through the rain to hear Mr Kent, and returns on the morrow to Manchester, feeling unwell. On 23 September, John M'Kenzie, who for the last year has been helping with the *Gospel Standard*, comes over from Preston and dines with him at the Gadsbys, and he comes over again on the Tuesday evening following, 26 September, when my father preaches his 'Leper' sermon 'fr. Lev. 13:45, 46; Kershaw, M'Kenzie, Higson and Nunn there'. On the next day he leaves Manchester at 6.40 a.m. by railway for Birmingham, catches the Leicester coach at 12, and arrives in that town at 6 p.m. The next day, having called on Mr Freer, the lawyer, for advice about cutting off the entail and selling the Lindfield farm, he preaches in the evening from Psalm 42:11.

On that very day, 28 September, though my father does not hear the sad news immediately, the lady he had loved in Ireland has died from the effects of her confinement, '*A.P. mortua est*', thereby removing the last obstacle, if only a sentimental one, to his marriage. On 1 October, the Lord's day, he preaches in Stamford: 'Mr and Mrs K. there in aftn.'

On 3 October, a fine warm day, Mr de M. drives him over to Gretford, where he inspects the marble tablet in the chancel to his grandfather, the Rev. Peter Lafargue, and interviews the wife of his new tenant, Mrs Bland. The little 60-acre farm of deep black soil is within a walk of Gretford, and had been bought cheap by Elias Lafargue, the rector, about 1740, when the value of the Fens had hardly been discovered. A few miles off, across the dead level Fen, stands the ancient tower of Crowland Abbey, which I climbed one fine October day many years ago and witnessed a sight I shall never forget. A strong west wind was driving fleece-like clouds across a bright blue sky, and on the level plain below as far as eye could reach the smoke from a thousand twitch-fires was being similarly chased over the bright green fields. It was a scene which told of happy and profitable industry.

But to go back to Stamford and the October of 1837. Mrs Keal has again come over from Oakham to stay with her eldest brother, James Tiptaft, of Tinwell Lodge, while my father is still with Mr de M. He sees her every day and we can guess the main subject of their talk.

Then on Friday, 20 October: 'Came from Stamfd. to Om.; dear S.L.K. there; *amplexus ut antea* (embraced as before).' From then until he again leaves Oakham for Allington on 22 November the Diary, as you might expect, is almost blank. Back once more at Allington he stays there for the short remainder of the year pleasantly occupied in writing the Annual Address for the *Gospel Standard*, in pruning Mr Parry's roses and currant bushes, and in beginning to commit to paper his sermon *Winter afore Harvest*. He even works at it on Monday, Christmas Day, after preaching in the morning to a good congregation. Almost the last entry in the Diary on 30 December is 'wrote *au soir* to J.G., chiefly about new work'. So ends on a note of pleasant anticipation one of the most pregnant years of my dear father's life.

13: Rutland Terrace and the *Gospel Standard*

THE CLAIM MAY BE A BOLD ONE, BUT I HAVE HEARD IT prophesied that in centuries to come that delectable spot, Rutland Terrace, Stamford, will be linked as closely in many hearts with the honoured memory of J. C. Philpot, as are the house and garden at Olney with that of William Cowper, and poor John Bunyan's with Bedford Gaol. For it was in one or other of its twenty houses that he spent the twenty-five most arduous, most fruitful, and I grieve to add, most maligned and calumniated years of his life. Thither came chosen friends, ministers, and visitors from overseas. From there his words, born of fervent prayer and spiritual meditation,[1] were carried far and wide. And there in his hours of ease toward the close of day he dictated the letters included in *The Seceders*, vol. II. These were all written before I was born, but perhaps I may be allowed to reproduce here my memory of a certain winter evening some years later in my parents' lives, when I, as the youngest of the four little 'trials' whom God had sent them for their good, was a rather privileged person, and perhaps unduly spoilt.

In the large first-floor room at No. 10, known as the Library, the curtains have been drawn and the shaded reading-lamp lit. It is past my bedtime, but on promising to be as quiet as a mouse I am allowed to sit on the floor and play by myself for

[1] 'Spiritual meditation', he contended, 'so needs the immediate and sustained help and power of the blessed Spirit, that it can be neither begun nor carried on without Him. In it the soul is not as a fish in a pool which may alike swim or sleep without any sensible difference, but like a bird in the air which, unless its flight be continually sustained by the exertion of its wings, at once drops to the ground.'—*Meditations*, First Series, p. 155.

an extra ten minutes in a corner near the fire. A few feet away my mother is seated at a writing-table, pen in hand and the lamp by her side, while my father, with crossed knees from his armchair by the fire, dictates one of his prized letters to some dear distant friend. In the flicker of the burning logs I see a strip of white stocking and an evening shoe beating slow time to the rhythm of his dictation. 'Little pitchers have long ears', and suddenly, as my father pauses in the middle of a sentence to let my mother catch him up, I am tempted to finish it for him in my childish treble. Every practised speaker has a store of set phrases, small change, with which he will tail off one sentence while thinking of the next. From having sat through so many of my father's sermons I happen to know most of his favourite 'tags', if I may call them so, and on this occasion I am not, I think, very wide of the mark. 'Hold your tongue, child', cries my mother, as crossly as she knows how, but my father, so far from administering the snubbing I deserve, enters into the spirit of the game, and takes the wind out of my conceit by ending his sentence in a way that no one else would have thought of. In his Letters he has sometimes painted himself in such dark colours, that I have ventured to put in this little bit of 'high light', to show what a dear indulgent father he could be.

*

But to go back for a moment to years before I was born. We have seen how on a certain wintry day early in 1837 he was driven in a hired fly from that house in St Mary's Street, Stamford, which I always think of as 'Melancholy Hall', to my grandparents' cheery home in Oakham Market Place. Now as he had to pay a shilling at Tinwell toll-gate, we happen to know that the driver, instead of leaving the town, as he should have done, by Scotgate, took his fare down through what he probably called 'The Shippens', i.e. the Sheep Market, and then up again by Castle Hill and past that large untidy mound, that centuries-old children's playground, beneath which had lain all that the Lancastrian army had left of St Peter's church and graveyard in 1461, until it was fenced and planted in my time to receive a Russian gun from the Crimea. Thence it is only a short distance to the gap in the town wall where formerly had stood St Peter's gate, through which the old turnpike-road led, not to Oakham, but through Tinwell and Ketton across the hills of little Rutland to Uppingham, Leicester and the west. It may be said without exaggeration that to pass through that gap even a century ago was not unlike leaving a prison or a pesthouse for health and freedom.[1]

Suddenly through the fly window on his left my father's eye could range across the snow-clad Welland valley to the leafless woods on its distant slopes. On his right he saw, I know not whether for the first time, a long row of neat new houses, separated from the paved sidewalk by little gardens, and faced with a light fawn-coloured free-stone almost fresh from the stone-cutter's saw. Rutland Terrace! And for him, I believe, it was almost a case of love at first sight! It was called Rutland Terrace because it is almost within sight of that diminutive county, and it is happy in having been built at a period when English architects had not yet lost their sense of proportion or their preference for unadorned simplicity.[2] Architecturally,

[1] Like many other country towns, Stamford had not then, nor for long after, either cemetery or main drainage. Served by ancient cess-pools, it was never free from typhoid fever, and faces all pitted with smallpox were far from uncommon. Meanwhile, except in St Martin's, which had its own cemetery, the little churchyards were crammed.

[2] Mr Wickham has pointed out in *The Villages of England* (London, 1932), p. 34, how it is the oolite quarries close around Stamford which have given 'that dignified city' the highest rank in architectural quality. 'An excellent tradition has been maintained in its churches, inns, and domestic buildings from the time of the spire of St Mary's right down to the nineteenth century.'

indeed, it may easily have reminded him of his Fellow's rooms in the middle of the raised terrace at Worcester College, which dated from not so many years earlier, and had the same round-headed ground floor windows and were faced with the same plain sawn free-stone. But in contrast to the cloistered and shaded peace of an Oxford college, Rutland Terrace faced the sun, was open to the winds, and, standing as it did on a highway, saw farmers' gigs by the dozen, and horses, sheep and cattle by the score driven past it to Friday market, while on Sunday mornings the town-dwellers chose its sidewalk for their favourite after-church promenade. On other days it could be as quiet as anyone could wish.

My father, I should say, had special reasons for an interest in the place, for Rutland Terrace had been built partly on an ancient bowling-green which had belonged to his grandfather, the Rev. Peter Lafargue, and had formed part of his mother's inheritance. Indeed the narrow thoroughfare between Rutland Terrace and the town wall was known in my young days as Bowling-Green Lane. My grandmother had sold the little property in 1813, when she was hard pressed by doctors' bills at Ripple Rectory, and my father was an ailing boy of eleven, menaced by the fate which was soon to carry off his two young sisters. The rest of the site must have been a sloping bank of stony waste wedged in between the Tinwell Road and that prehistoric 'By-pass', which we always called the Back-way, because it took one to chapel without going through the town, though its proper name is West Street, until it crosses Scotgate and is continued as our familiar North Street, to join the main route again beyond the town. Hence most of the houses in Rutland Terrace have their back gates on a much higher level than the front ones, and stone steps lead up to them from the little back gardens. For us children those back gates spelt liberty, so we will return to them later.

On its being providentially decided for him that he was to live at Stamford, my father had lost no time in selling his Sussex farm and investing the proceeds in No. 10 Rutland Terrace, the only one then in the market, but it was let on a long lease, and he did not get possession until the year of the great comet, 1858. Meanwhile he rented successively No. 15 and No. 14, but my young memories are nearly all of No. 10.

Rutland Terrace stands high above the Welland Valley and enjoys an unimpeded view. Leaning over the balcony of the library at No. 10, one could imagine — a child can imagine anything — that one was in the royal box of an enormous green amphitheatre, the floor of which was the mile-long dead-level stretch of Stamford common meadow curving away on the right to the waterfall and Tinwell mill, both out of sight, while the opposite tiers across the valley, which a child could people with crowds and banners, were for an older eye only the thickly wooded slopes and hay-fields of Northamptonshire, fringe of the ancient Rockingham Forest where King John loved to chase the deer. From St Martin's high-pinnacled church-tower rising above the houses on the extreme left to that of Easton on the far right, standing high upon its distant hill, all in my youth was green woodland with nothing to arrest the eye but the four turrets of Wothorpe ruins, still capped with lead. I like to picture my father on some fine May morning leaving his Hebrew Old Testament for a while, stepping out on to his sunny balcony, and inhaling from all that far-flung green loveliness a sense of peace.

The view has long since been ruined as a view by that intruder, the Midland Railway and its red-brick monstrosities, but when my parents first settled in Rutland Terrace in 1839, instead of little local trains puffing and crawling at intervals along the valley, they could watch on their extreme left an endless procession of gay stage-coaches and travelling chariots being carefully steered up or down that steep bit of the Great North Road just beyond the rococo lodge gates of Burghley Park. Afterwards for the best part of a century Stamford was blissfully secluded from all through traffic, and we schoolboys on a fine half-holiday would sometimes tramp the four miles to Tallington just to see 'the Flying Scotsman' race past. But since the coming of the motor car, that primitive highway, the Great North Road, has recovered its ancient use, and Stamford a share of its old importance.

At one time my father had thoughts of moving his growing family to a beautiful old house in St George's Square, not many doors from where he had stayed with Mr de Merveilleux, but as, for one thing, it had no view, he fortunately gave up the idea, and the *Gospel Standard* continued to be edited from Rutland Terrace and published from Bouverie Street, whence, as old issues tell, it found its way to private soldiers shivering in Crimean trenches, or sweltering before the gates of Delhi; to lonely men living in shacks on the Ballarat gold-fields, or on remote Australian sheep-farms; to lovers of truth in new American townships; while at home it was sold in ever-increasing numbers.

No account of my father would be complete without some mention of the Tinwell Road, which formerly led past Rutland Terrace straight into the open country. Now it is lined with modern villas and its ancient peace has fled. But on nine days out of ten, as soon as his long morning's task was done, my father would put on his cloak and tall hat, issue from his front gate, turn to the right, and within less than a hundred yards would find the quiet that his soul required for silent meditation, if, to borrow one of his favourite expressions, he was not to prove a dry breast to the many thousands who looked to him for spiritual food. The broad pathway on the right was raised some five feet above the dusty white road and commanded a wide view over the valley. There were four or five posts at one point to keep stray sheep and cattle off it, when driven in by the score to fair or market. On some days he would only go as far as 'the posts' and back. More usually he would extend his walk to Tinwell toll-bar, which crowned the gentle rise and marked the entry into Rutland, with its elm-bordered lanes. On his good days he would venture into the valley as far as what we called 'Pa's Tree', a big elm which happened to stand out in the middle of the path, and lent itself admirably to the game of 'hide-and-seek'. Very occasionally he would get even as far as the pretty model village of Tinwell with its old stocks under the trees in front of the little church, whither James Tiptaft, my grandmother's eldest brother (b. 1792), came down from Tinwell Lodge to worship with his wife and family, and where one of his handsome daughters led the singing and played the barrel-organ which ground out one or other of its half-dozen hymn tunes. Sometimes my father would take one of his children with him, and give a botany lesson, picking a wild flower and teaching his pupil to examine and name all its distinctive parts. Or he would thrill one with the graphic story of Sukey Harley, as he had thrilled the readers of the *Gospel Standard* ten years earlier.[1]

There was nothing, I should mention, that he mistrusted more than infant piety. For long he was opposed to Sunday schools, till he had to give way before the general consensus of his followers. But he did not cease to insist that children should never be taught or allowed to use the language of appropriation, to sing, for instance, 'Rock of ages, cleft for *me*'; or, '*My* Jesus hath done all things well'. Herein he was quite logical. For though by early influence and example you can bring up a child to be a little patriot, a little Catholic, a

[1] *Gospel Standard*, May 1849. *Reviews*, Vol. I, p. 5.

little Calvinist, a little Bolshevist, and perhaps even a little 'citizen of the world', no power on earth, he would have maintained, can make him a child of God unless his name has been written in the Lamb's book of life. He took care that we, his children, attended the means of grace, and never missed chapel or family prayers, but he did not expect us to be anything but little heathen. We had, it is true, to be well-behaved little heathen. If not, we got the stick, or its equivalent. Outside the front gate of Rutland Terrace it behoved us to be clean and tidy and well-conducted. But outside the back gate we could romp as we pleased. There grubby hands and towzled hair brought no reproach. Fortunately we had 'the drying-ground' to play in.

Mention must be made at this point of Samuel Lightfoot, described by my father as a 'truly good man and an ornament to his Christian profession'. His toy and china shop and hair-dressing saloon, if such it could be called, was situated in the short, narrow thoroughfare known as Maiden Lane. He was a short, spare man, with a fresh complexion, very blue eyes and a musical voice. In my time he had been succeeded by a lanky son, young Sam, whom we children disliked as much as we liked his father. Those were the days when a country hairdresser had a busy, healthy, and not unremunerative life, largely occupied as it was in 'waiting upon gentlemen at their own residences'. Stamford was surrounded by baronial mansions, country-seats and village rectories, where Samuel Lightfoot had found his work sufficiently well paid to enable him to retire in favour of his son at an age comparatively young, and henceforth to devote himself to the care of North Street chapel and the needs of its poorer hearers. In my day it was young Sam who came at times to Rutland Terrace to clip my father's abundant hair. We all knew when he had been because for the rest of that day my father, sensitive to cold as he was, kept

F

his head covered with a red bandanna handkerchief. He had not discovered, as I have, how a cold douche to the head immediately after the clip will forestall that sense of chilliness.

Every other Friday morning, it should be remembered, my father took train for Oakham and did not return until mid-day on the following Wednesday. So our Lord's days became classed as Preaching Sundays and Reading Sundays. On the former, vehicles by the dozen and pedestrians by the score came in from the surrounding country, so that, with the town dwellers, the chapel was crammed, whereas on 'Reading Sundays' it was little more than half full. Usually it was Mr Scott who occupied the reading-desk, and sent us to sleep with his monotonous drone; so that one heartily welcomed the rare occasions on which Samuel Lightfoot with his musical voice replaced him. At Rutland Terrace, Reading Sunday was invariably followed by 'washing day', and on the Wednesday my father returned to a house which in his absence had been cleaned from top to bottom, and from that moment we all had to behave and 'study to be quiet'.

When my father came at last into possession of No. 10, his first care was to build a wash-house in the back garden, and a little lean-to greenhouse with a large tank to collect the rain-water beneath it, in place of the old water-butt which had served that purpose at No. 14. If the little greenhouse proved a boon to my father, as a place where he could find some relaxation when it was too cold or too wet for his usual walk, to my mother it was a source of unending interest. Like her father, she was a born gardener. She installed her own little propagating frame, kept at the right temperature by cheap ingenious devices, and she grudged no trouble to make her seedlings thrive. The seven-foot hollyhocks in the little front garden which one year were the envy of all our neighbours had cost her nothing but the price of a gallon or two of Colza oil.

But the wash-house, with its ample supply of rain-water, brought still greater comfort to her thrifty soul, for with washing at home, both house and body linen seemed never to wear out. Every other Monday, when my father was safe out of the way at Oakham, the washerwoman came and kept the maids busy carrying off the clothes to dry. Across the Back-way, between a cornfield and a rickyard and chicken-run, was that oblong strip of land enclosed by loose stone walls and entered by a heavy creaking gate, known as 'the drying-ground'. Except on washing-days we children had it to our-selves, to tend our little gardens, devise new little games, and rifle the strawberry bed. In its time the drying-ground was called on to play many parts. One day it would figure as the threshing-floor of Boaz, that mighty man of wealth. Another day it would be the courtyard and well of Cawnpore, the tragic details of which had recently been told us by our father at the tea-table, and had lost none of their grisly horror in the telling.

*

Rutland Terrace, as we have remarked already, was the name inseparably linked with the *Gospel Standard*. We have seen how in 1837 John Gadsby was constantly urging my father to contribute something to the infant magazine. In the previous year he had enlisted the help of John M'Kenzie, a young Scotsman, who was pastor of a Particular Baptist Chapel at Preston. Eventually it was the combined but curiously con-trasted gifts of these three men, John Gadsby, John M'Kenzie and my father, which, as soon as each had fallen into his appointed place—for they were all new to their work—not only saved the *Gospel Standard* from imminent extinction but, under strict and conscientious editorship, made it a rich storehouse of that divine teaching usually known as the doctrines of grace, and of authentic spiritual experience.

For eleven years then, from 1836 to 1847, it was M'Kenzie who carefully chose the contents of the *Gospel Standard*, who stood, as it were, at the passages of Jordan and slaughtered all contributions which could not frame to pronounce the Word of truth aright. John Gadsby tells us that M'Kenzie returned the MSS. which had been sent him in three packets marked 1. Good; 2. Moderate; 3. Rejected. No. 1 he used first, and if he had not enough to make up, he, John Gadsby himself, selected from No. 2. But my father, when he took over the task, left him no such choice. Nos. 2 and 3 found their way into the wastepaper basket. He sent back only Nos. 1, and was very sparing even of those, so that poor John Gadsby 'was often, to the very last, distressed for the lack of Nos. 2'; while sometimes my father, perhaps after two laborious Lord's day services, had to sit up half the night and write something to fill the gap. But it is due to his unfailing vigilance, following that of M'Kenzie, in excluding everything which was not of permanent and un-ageing value that the first thirty-five volumes of the *Gospel Standard* read almost as freshly now as on their day of issue.

My father, I may explain, had the nervous poetic temperament without the poetic gift. He was what the Germans call a *Dichter*, that is to say, a man who writes or speaks from his heart as well as his head. Hence his sermons and reviews do not 'date' and can still be read with profit. For the head speaks merely for a season, but the heaven-taught heart for all time. Prose was his natural instrument, and few writers of his day wielded it to better purpose. His writing carries the reader along with it; so too did his preaching. A Stamford lady who was far from sharing his views, when taken to task for going so often to hear him, replied, 'But he's so interesting!'

[164]

In these early years of his ministry, my father's responsibility for much that went into the *Gospel Standard*, his unswerving contention for true heartfelt religion, and his unqualified condemnation of all its counterfeits, exposed him continually to virulent abuse, calumny and misrepresentation. In one year alone, as he told a close friend, as many as thirty pamphlets were published against him. He was himself partly to blame, for, as he admitted in later years, his youthful zeal often outran discretion and led him into mistakes. He was confessedly a critic, and his natural inclination was to pick holes rather than to praise. And he found so few he could wholeheartedly commend. Hence ministers to whom he had turned the cold shoulder, writers whose effusions he had thrown into his wastepaper basket, professors whose self-righteous withers he had wrung, and many thin-skinned persons whom he had unwittingly offended, all ranged themselves against him. 'To be honest', he writes, 'is to raise up powerful and bitter enemies, to wound and alienate friends, to make oneself a mark for arrows of slander and reproach.' Yet all the while the circulation of the *Gospel Standard* was going up by leaps and bounds. 'In villages and hamlets far distant from any preached gospel, among churches and congregations where the ministry is a dry breast, in the sick room whence persecuting relatives banish the Christian minister or friend, even in foreign lands where truth is neither preached nor known, in the Australian hut or Canadian loghouse, a piece from Rusk, or a letter from Huntington, not to mention living correspondents, may be a messenger of mercy.'[1]

It was in his Annual Addresses that my father entered into the most intimate relations with his readers. The few extracts which follow are selected from those which he wrote between 1844 and 1849:

[1] *Gospel Standard*, 1849, p. 3.

'What mostly do we reap as the fruit of our editorial labours? Weariness of body and anxiety of mind. . . . If we would exercise honestly our own judgment, we must create ourselves constant sources of pain . . . sharpen men's eyes to our own failings and shortcomings, and stand in that painful, isolated spot where one is more feared than loved. As Editors, we are professedly judges of others; and we need not say how this draws the eyes of men to every failing or mark of incompetence, and through what a magnifying glass wounded self-love views every blemish in the hand that hurts it.' – 1844, p. 4.

'A spirit of delusion seems to us widely prevalent. . . . A carnal confidence, a dead assurance, a presumptuous claim, a daring mimicry of the spirit of adoption – who that has eyes or heart does not see and feel the wide spread of this gigantic evil? . . . No brokenness of heart, no tenderness of conscience, no spirituality of mind, no heavenly affections, no prayerfulness and watchfulness, no godly devotedness of life, no self-denial and crucifixion, no humility or contrition, no separation from the world, no communion with the Lord of life and glory – in a word, none of the blessed graces and fruits of the Spirit attend this hardened assurance. On the contrary, levity, jesting, pride, covetousness, self-exaltation, and often gross self-indulgence, with love of strong drink and idle gossip, are evidently stamped upon many, if not most, of these hardened professors.' – 1845, p. 2.

'But what is our leading object, the mark at which we aim, the goal towards which we run? It is to contend for the power and experience of truth in the conscience – for that, and that only, which God the Spirit has revealed in the Word, and which He works by His divine operation in the souls of His elect family. This comprehends the whole of revealed truth; this embraces the work of the Spirit, from the first pang of guilt to the last note of praise that dies upon the lips of the expiring saint.' — 1846, p. 1.

'What minister of Jesus Christ has not seen warm friends become bitter foes? What gospel church has not found its greatest troubles arise from the perverseness and frowardness of those whom they could not cut off as altogether destitute of grace? Who wounded most our dear departed friend Gadsby, and, as the poor old man said, well-nigh broke his heart? Some whom, with all their treatment of him, he still believed were partakers of grace. Hart has expressed to the life the path of the Christian: "From sinner and from saint he meets with many a blow." What spiritual reader of our pages cannot from his own painful experience say, "This witness is true"?' — 1847, p. 5.

'A simple, childlike, confiding trust in the God of all our mercies, the Object of all our desires, and the Source of all our consolations — how precious, how desirable a blessing! Instead of trembling at every leaf, of anxiously fearing approaching trials, of looking droopingly forward to the next day's dawn lest the morn should bring forth some new trial, blessed with this grace, we should trust and not be afraid of any evil tidings (Ps. 112:7), nor add to the real sufferings of the day the imaginary sufferings of the morrow.' — 1848, p. 4.

'If our pages are idly read, listlessly gaped over, and then carelessly thrown aside, how does the *Gospel Standard* differ from a newspaper? If no good be done by it: no sad heart comforted, no drooping heart revived, no doubting heart encouraged, no erring heart reproved, no cold heart warmed, no hard heart melted; if it convey no reproof, correction, instruction, or consolation; if it mislead instead of guide, harden instead of soften, engender carnality, worldliness and death, instead of spirituality, heavenly-mindedness and life, why should we trouble ourselves any more with its publication?

[167]

. . . But because it is our belief that good has been done, and is doing by us, we are encouraged to persevere.'—1849, p. 4.

Meanwhile even his most intimate friends hardly realized how severe was the strain upon him, and how he longed sometimes to escape from the arrows of his foes. 'Why have I so many enemies?' he asks Thomas Godwin, one of his ministerial friends. 'Other ministers pass along untouched, but book after book comes out against me, as if they would sink me outright. Alas! how soon the heart sinks down when trouble arises, and I could not help wishing I had lived and died in the Church of England. I thought I might have been quiet there, and need not have preached at all.' 'If I were to be satisfied with a dry doctrinal religion,' he tells another correspondent, 'I should be let alone. But because I contend for the power, some seem almost as if they would pull me to pieces. And if I know nothing of experience, why do I contend for it? Why did I not stay in the Church of England, where I might, but for conscience' sake, have been this day, without let or molestation? . . . But all their attacks only give me fresh errands to the Throne of Grace.'

After the untimely death of John M'Kenzie on 12 August 1849 my father had to undertake the 'united and entire management' of the *Gospel Standard*, while leaving the advertisement wrapper more or less under the control of John Gadsby. For this work he was supremely well fitted, and the magazine enjoyed a thriving existence. It was no mere supplement to the speaking voice, but a ministry in its own right and, within its own limits, an extremely potent one. Its aim was to feed the 'little flock' with 'the finest of the wheat' and 'with honey out of the rock to satisfy them'. Undoubtedly it fulfilled its purpose.

14: In death not divided

IN A PREVIOUS CHAPTER I DESCRIBED THE CHARACTER-
istics of the ministry of William Tiptaft in the Abingdon
district, and explained how, after his secession from the
Established Church, a chapel was built in which his numerous
hearers could be accommodated. He too experiences to the
full the world's stolid indifference, unbelief, and self-com-
placency, accompanied as it is by its bitterness towards the
doctrines and experiences which he preached. Added to this
is his sorrow that so few among the truly godly really live up
to the faith which they profess. From the end of the year 1833
onward a new note is heard in his letters. He is 'tried in his
soul in various ways'. He feels himself 'so unfit for a pastor'.
His 'preaching tries him very much'. It is a terrible task 'to
stand up between an ever-living God and never-dying souls'.
'All things are very puzzling and no one more than myself to
myself; for I am a mystery indeed.' 'I am driven into corners
and often wonder where the scene will end.' As with other
extroverts, when he begins to be introspective, his difficulties
become too great for his powers of adjustment. And yet he
goes on, year after year, touring the country, wherever he can
find a pulpit or a barn to preach in, as if, to quote the verdict
of an observant friend, his constitution had been of oak, and
not, as it really was, of deal.

At last the overdriven body rises up in fierce rebellion
against the soul. Unbearable pains assail him, and drive him
from the field. His splanchnic plexus, the knot of sensitive
nerves at the pit of the stomach, gives him no peace. He has to
take refuge with my grandparents, there to be nursed, if pos-

sible, back to health. The months drag past and the fear is that he will die, 'gradually sink', to quote my father, who was witness of his misery, 'worn out by his complaint and the toils and labours of his past ministry'. As he was staying at Oakham during this time there is a long gap between his letters, and a veil is mercifully drawn for us over his suffering.

The year and more of bodily rest has given the soul a chance of regaining its mastery, but it is a chastened soul, which never quite regains its old assurance. 'He had been brought down from the mount,' again to quote my father, 'that he might learn experimentally to walk in the valley of humiliation where the best taught and most deeply led of the Lord's living family are usually found.'

After that there is another long gap in the correspondence. For now that my grandparents have definitely ranged themselves on his side, there is the less need to admonish them; nay, it is he himself who now stands most in need of encouragement. In spite of much darkness of mind and bondage of spirit, he has to resume his preaching. He has put his hand to the plough and cannot, dare not look back. He has moments of comfort and relief, when he is able blessedly to feel that the Lord is on his side. But on the whole the four years that follow his illness are years of trial and perplexity. Then, when least looked for, there comes a marvellous deliverance, and the long series of letters ends in a splendid song of praise:

'I have now something to relate, in which, I trust, you and the other friends at Oakham will feel interested, and will be glad to hear; and may the Lord make it a blessing, and may He have all the praise! It is a new strain for me to begin with: "My heart is inditing a good matter; I speak of the things which I have made touching the King; my tongue is the pen of a ready writer."

'After talking over the proceedings of the day with four

friends, I retired (on Lord's day evening)[1] to bed in a comfortable state of mind, feeling thankful that the Lord had brought me through a trying day, concerning which I had been much exercised, and trusting the Lord had blest the Word to some that day through such a worm as I felt myself to be, as well as owning His own ordinance, to which we had been attending. When I knelt down to offer up a few words by the bedside, I felt my soul drawn out to God, and humbled low before Him with a sense of my sins; but as soon as I was in bed I began to feel a melting of heart, and a sweet sense of God's love to my soul, which immediately made my tears flow; and the Lord sweetly began to apply precious promises to my soul with unction and power, and to such an extent as I have never been blest with before. In fact I have never experienced any such blessed manifestation and sweet deliverance, though I have been blessed at different times that I can mention; but they were far short of this sweet blessing to my soul; and the savour of it sweetly abides with me still, but I am afraid of losing it, or of being robbed of it.

'When the promises began to flow into my soul, these words came with as great power, and as often as any: "Awake and sing, ye that dwell in dust; for thy dew is as the dew of herbs"; and again and again: "I have blotted out, as a thick cloud, thy trangressions, and, as a cloud, thy sins: return unto Me; for I have redeemed thee"; "I will honour them that honour Me"; "He that hath My commandments, and keepeth them, he it is that loveth Me: and he that loveth Me shall be loved of My Father, and I will love him, and will manifest Myself to him." I did sweetly experience this manifestation of love to my soul; and I said to the blessed Lord, "Let Him kiss me with the kisses of His mouth", "for His mouth is most sweet". The

[1] On this Lord's day (29 January 1843) he had baptized thirteen women and ten men.

promises flowed into my soul, and my tears flowed so fast that I
soon began to water my couch with tears of joy and not of
sorrow. I lay till between twelve and one o'clock in this blessed
state, and then fell asleep, for about two hours, and awoke in
a delightful frame, the Lord blessing my soul again, till I
had to restrain myself from crying aloud. I did not go to sleep
again, but lay awake, blessing and praising God for His goodness and mercy to my soul, with debasing views of myself,
and with exalted views of the blessed Jesus, having communion
and fellowship with Him in His agony and sufferings. But
during my soul-enjoyment I kept saying at times, "Is it real,
Lord? Is it real, Lord?" I wanted to know whether it was real.
I asked myself whether I was willing to die, and I felt I was;
and if it were the Lord's will, I was willing to die without
telling anyone of His great goodness to my soul; for the Lord's
will was my will. I asked myself whether I would rather have
a large bag of gold or this blessing, and I felt a large bag of
gold was no more to me than a large bag of pebbles, compared to the Lord's rich blessing. These words came to my
mind sweetly again and again:

> "Now will I tell to sinners round
> What a dear Saviour I have found."

And Hart's hymn:

> "Blest Spirit of truth, eternal God," etc.,

was sweet to my soul.

'I went up and told J.K. early in the morning, and could not
refrain from crying, and could scarcely shave myself through
shedding tears so fast. I shed more tears last night than I have
shed for years, for my tears do not flow so easily as many
people's do. These words came with power: "Sing, O ye
heavens; for the Lord hath done it", etc.; and also: "Though

your sins be as scarlet, they shall be as white as snow; though they be red like crimson, they shall be as wool." This has been to my soul "a feast of fat things, of fat things full of marrow, and of wines on the lees well refined"; for "the vision is yet for an appointed time, but at the end it shall speak, and not lie: though it tarry wait for it, because it will surely come, it will not tarry".

'You, as well as others, know I have had to wait, and have been much tried, because the Lord has not blest me more with His presence and manifestations of His love, though He has given me a few sips by the way, both in preaching and at a throne of grace, and in times of need and temptation. But I have known to my sorrow what it is to sit in the dust, almost without hope whether the Lord would ever put a new song in my mouth. These words were brought again and again: "Bless the Lord, O my soul, and all that is within me, bless His holy name; bless the Lord, O my soul, and forget not all His benefits: who forgiveth all thine iniquities; who healeth all thy diseases; who redeemeth thy life from destruction; who crowneth thee with loving-kindness and tender mercies." I have gone on in the ministry ready to halt, with sorrow before me, with my soul much discouraged because of the way; and had not the Lord given me seals to my ministry and testimonies now and then to my soul, surely I must have fainted by the way. If the blessing had come twelve hours sooner, some one else must have preached and baptized, for I could have done neither, through blessing, praising, and crying for joy. Very many of my hearers would have said, it was not enthusiasm in the bud but in the flower, for they are strangers to such feelings. "The heart knoweth his own bitterness; and a stranger doth not intermeddle with his joy." And how clearly did I see David's wisdom in saying, "Come and hear, all ye that fear God, and I will declare what He hath done for my soul." David

[173]

well knew, that if they did not know a "secret" in religion, they would not be able to understand a work of grace upon the soul. I have been long kept upon short commons, and I have had great murmurings and rebellion respecting it, and now the Lord is pleased to lead my soul into green pastures; but how long I am to be favoured, I know not, but this I know, I feel grateful for what the Lord has granted me, and I love Him, and can bless His holy name. "O that men would praise the Lord for His goodness, and for His wonderful works to the children of men!"

'I have been led to know my vileness, and to feel much of the depravity of my heart, so as to be sensibly a poor, lost, ruined sinner. Sometimes I have envied the brute creation, and at times I have thought God would strike me dead, being sensible of so much sin in my heart. I felt sure I had but little grace, if I had any at all; and my mind has been much tried respecting the formation of a church here, seeing it a grievous thing that the ordinances of God's house should be slighted and neglected year after year by those who, I believe, were the proper persons to attend to them. I could, therefore, see the need of church order and government much better than I could see in any way my fitness to be a pastor. So I was in great straits, and looked forward to the ordinance next Lord's day with much exercise and trial of mind, having to administer it in my darkness of soul, and knowing also that there is such a thing as eating and drinking unworthily, and that such "eat and drink damnation (or condemnation) to themselves, not discerning the Lord's body".

'On Friday evening I was with two friends who were speaking of the Lord's manifestations to their souls; but I was dumb, and could say nothing, and felt as if I could not possibly stand in the position I was placed in, being so dark, shut up, and tried. On Saturday, too, I felt much darkness and trial of mind, but I little thought that God's great goodness and mercy were so soon to be manifested to my soul. I have had sips, but now my cup is full, and even runneth over. In the days of adversity I have considered how the scene would end, but now in the day of prosperity my soul is joyful. "I will be glad and rejoice in Thy mercy, for Thou hast considered my trouble; Thou hast known my soul in adversities, and hast not shut me up into the hand of the enemy; Thou hast set my feet in a large room." "The blessing of the Lord, it maketh rich, and He addeth no sorrow with it." The Lord continues to bless my soul with His love, and Christ is precious; and I am sure the Lord's spiritual blessings to my soul do not lead to worldliness and licentiousness, but to deadness to the world and to separation in spirit from it. Real faith works by love, and Christ is truly precious, and there is no true victory over the world but through this blessed experience, known and felt in the soul; and love to Jesus is accompanied with love to the brethren, and with earnest and sincere prayers for the children of God. "They shall prosper that love Zion." Before this blessing I looked forward to the ordinance of the Lord's Supper as a man would who had a great payment to make, and had not wherewith to pay; he wishes that there was no such engagement, or that the time was rather distant; and now I can look upon it as the man would upon the payment, if any one had given him all or more than all the money.'

But for years before this culminating experience he had already spent his strength and strained his health in finding and calling out God's chosen people from a careless and licentious world:

'The Lord only knows', he writes, 'what hidden ones there are in your dark little town and county, and He will appoint some means to bring His banished ones home.' His solemn conviction, which only deepened with the years, that he himself was one of these *means*, not as ordained by a bishop, but as *appointed* directly by the Most High, was what sustained him through a life of unremitting toil, tortured though he was by an awful sense of his responsibility. In the vestry before service, we are told,[1] he would pace the floor; sitting in the pulpit, while the hymn before his sermon was being sung, he would appear to be in agony. Then he would rise to his feet, shaking his head and wringing his hands. Unfit as he was—ignorant as he was—unworthy as he was, to stand up between the everlasting God and never-dying souls, he would pray most earnestly, that God would give His people a spirit of prayer for him who was about to address them. 'Oh! grant him seals to his ministry and souls for his hire.'

So wholly absorbed was William Tiptaft in his sacred mission, so rich and urgent had eternal things become to him, that he never opened a newspaper, and seldom any book except the Bible, and he knew little and cared less about what was happening in the world around him. It is related of him that once, when travelling by coach to preach, he came to a town where bells were ringing, flags flying, and people by the thousand thronging under triumphal arches. To his enquiry, a fellow-traveller, who had come miles to share in the spectacle, replied that they were there to do honour to the great Duke of Wellington. "Oh! indeed', said William Tiptaft in an unfeigned indifference, with which at this distant date some of us perhaps can sympathize.

Unlike my father, who, when once he had left the Church, kept his wide white shirt-front and snowy choker for the pulpit, and invariably on week-days put off everything parsonic and dressed like a gentleman of the period, with black stock, Gladstone collar, tweed trousers, white stockings and Oxford shoes, William Tiptaft always retained the black

[1] *Reminiscences of the late William Tiptaft* (Oxford, 1875).

broadcloth, white shirt-front and neat white tie which were the usual wear of evangelical parsons at that date. When he came to stay with us at Stamford, to fill the pulpit in my father's absence, he would walk up briskly from the station with his little black bag, and at the end of his visit walk as briskly away. While he was with us *The Times, Blackwood,* and *The Quarterly,* which my father always took in, had to be put out of sight, for he dreaded lest they should draw him away from Christ. Thirty years had passed since he had left the Church, and he had learnt much wisdom in the interval, but he always retained its uniform.

With 'living souls for his hire', he had an almost superstitious aversion from receiving any other. Nor would he, so long as his own small capital of four or five thousand pounds held out. Once when a devoted friend, hearing that he had wasted all his substance in giving help to others, sent him a cheque for £800, he would only accept it on condition that he might at once hand over half of it to the poor, and much of the residue, I believe, soon followed it.

What my father has called 'the greatest act of noble liberality and unwearied self-denial which even with all his sacrifices my friend ever made' has yet to be related.

Early in 1834 an almost penniless, rather feckless, and absolutely friendless young clergyman, named John Kay, who had been supported at college and up to his ordination by his elder brother, an Oxford Fellow, having for reasons of conscience resigned his curacy, seceded from the Church of England, and been in consequence cast off by all his relations, directed his steps to Abingdon, owing chiefly to what he had heard of William Tiptaft in the Kettering district, where his curacy had lain. Having listened to his story and been convinced that he had been guided in his steps by the power of God, William Tiptaft, to save the helpless youth from the workhouse, paid

[177]

his few debts, and offered him a small upper bedroom in the house where he himself was lodged. John Kay, with no other friend in the world to look to, except a rich but eccentric old uncle who would do nothing for him, had no alternative but to accept this kind and generous offer, although neither could have then foreseen how long the temporary arrangement would last.

'Though about two years later', writes my father, 'William Tiptaft moved into a somewhat better house, yet, beside the two bedrooms, he had but one sitting-room; and to share that year after year with one who had no claim upon him, but that of Christian brotherhood, was, I need not say, a sacrifice of his own comfort and privacy, such as no man but he, I believe, would or could have rendered. John Kay was a truly good man, and of a very amiable Christian spirit, but in many ways very eccentric, and being much afflicted in body was almost an invalid, and therefore trying always to live with. But for four-teen long years our friend lodged him, fed him, clothed him, and was to him indeed a father, a brother and a friend. It is true that some friends helped somewhat to bear with him the pecuniary expense, but all the load of having him continually in the same room was borne by his entertainer. Indeed, I think, had he not often gone out on his various preaching tours, and had not friends occasionally invited John Kay to pay them a visit, he himself with all his wonderful patience and kindness could scarcely have sustained it. . . . William Tiptaft was social naturally, and yet I know he much prized solitude and quiet and often spoke of them as profitable to his soul. John Kay was a pleasant and profitable companion, and by no means deficient in understanding or information. But men are but men, and to be always together should be angels, or glorified spirits, rather than fallen sons of Adam. For fourteen years, however, did William Tiptaft bear this load with a sinking income, and little prospect of any change.

'But in 1848 John Kay's uncle died and left him a handsome legacy. This unexpected intervention of the providence of God at once liberated our friend from his long, yet patiently endured burden, enabled the two friends to live apart, and restored to William Tiptaft his cherished privacy of life.'

After Tiptaft had more or less emerged from the trying period of doubts and fears and grievous self-distrust so fully recorded in his correspondence, and had been visited with the wonderful experience already mentioned, he settled down to a life of unremitting labour. During the twenty years which followed upon that 'signal blessing', he was, to quote my father's words, 'most abundant in the labours of the ministry, there being scarcely a town or village in any part of England where there was a people who knew and loved the truth, which he did not, as opportunity offered, willingly visit. The people of God at Manchester, Liverpool, Preston, Birmingham, Bradford, Helmsley, Lincoln, and many other places in the north; at Cirencester, Bath, Trowbridge, and almost innumerable chapels in Wilts in the west; Rochester, Maidstone, Faversham, in the east; Brighton, Chichester, and The Dicker in the south, with many other places which I cannot now name, all knew his voice, and loved and esteemed him for his bold and faithful testimony. Wherever he went his personal kindness, his freedom from all pride and pretence, his liberality to, and sympathy with the poor, his keen, pithy sentences, and his acknowledged godliness of life, added a weight to his public testimony such as few ministers in our day have, I believe, possessed.'

During the last year of his life his ministry was much hampered by a throat affliction which caused a chronic hoarseness and ultimately brought about his death. He felt the hindrance keenly and 'had great difficulty', writes my father, 'in bringing himself to the thought that he should suspend or even diminish his ministerial labours'. At Abingdon he preached his last sermon on 29 April 1863 from 2 Thess. 2:16–17. During the month following he 'supplied', as usual with him, at Gower Street Chapel, London, but the earnest advice of a metropolitan physician whom he consulted at this time convinced him that his ministry had now reached its close. July saw him again in his beloved Abingdon where, he assured his friends, 'he desired to live, to die, and to be buried'. In mid-August came the happy release, preceded by the glad testimony, 'My last moments are my best':

> When call'd to meet the King of dread,
> Should love compose my dying bed,
>   And grace my soul sustain,
> Then, ere I quit this mortal clay,
> I'll raise my fainting voice and say,
>   Let grace triumphant reign.

A friend said, 'Is that verse your mind now?' and he said, 'Yes'. It was no mere polite affirmation, for William Tiptaft always spoke the truth.

*

J. C. Philpot's ill-health prevented him from seeing his brother in Christ 'well laid in the grave', as he could have desired. He himself found it imperative only two months later to resign his pastorate at Oakham and Stamford. 'The climate of Stamford', he explained afterwards in the *Gospel Standard*, 'is peculiarly cold for its latitude and exposed to the east wind', and therefore 'unsuitable for my tender chest'. 'But besides this', he writes, 'I begin to find that my long and continued labours with the pen, with all the anxieties and cares of my position as editor of the *Standard*, all of which are added to the work of the ministry, were telling on my constitution. The wonder with me, and others who know me, is that I have not broken down before this. Other ministers, stouter and stronger than I, can rest when their work is done; but mine is ever going on, and only beginning when theirs is ending. Frequently after a Lord's day of hard ministerial labour, I have spent two hours and more writing before I went to bed – and hard writing too, for it was my "Meditations", or some subject which demanded much thought and most careful consideration from the Word of God and experience. Many a Lord's day I have worked with tongue or pen pretty well from morning to night, except at meals, and sometimes have scarcely had an hour of quiet rest. . . . I feel therefore that I must either stop in time, or go on and drop. Can anyone then rightly blame me if, with a family to provide for and, I hope, the church of God to think of, I do not sacrifice my life to stay at one post?'

From Stamford, then, he and his family – including two daughters and a son – removed to Croydon where he hoped a 'warmer and drier climate' would yield him benefit. There, too, Mr Francis Covell exercised a ministry after his own heart. A little over four years of life remained to him. Occasionally he preached. Writing, however, occupied most of his attention. 'That which cometh upon me daily, the care of all the churches' was at once the labour of his heart and his home. The appointed end came on 9 December 1869. His pen had remained busy until 21 November when an attack of bronchitis set in, and by 2 December he had become too ill to leave his bed. He acknowledged that goodness and mercy had followed him all the days of his life; and the comfortable state of his mind in the presence of death was evident from such ejaculations as could be caught at intervals: 'Better to die than to live! Mighty to save! mighty to save! I die in the faith I have preached and felt. The blood of Jesus Christ cleanseth us from *all* sin. Oh, if I could depart, and be with Christ, which is far better!

Praise the Lord; bless His holy name.' Then at the last he looked up earnestly, and closing his eyes said, 'Beautiful!' His wife asked: 'What is beautiful?' But he made no direct answer, only with failing voice said presently, 'Praise the Lord, O my soul!'

Appendix

Appendix

Philpot's letter to the Provost of Worcester College, Oxford

Stadhampton 28 *March* 1835

MR PROVOST: I beg leave to resign the Fellowship of Worcester College, to which I was elected in the year 1826. This step I am compelled to take because I can no longer with a good conscience continue a Minister or a Member of the Established Church.

After great and numerous trials of mind, I am, as I trust, led by the hand of God thus to separate myself from that corrupt and worldly system, called the Church of England. Her errors and corruptions, as well as her utter contrariety to a Gospel Church as revealed in the New Testament, have been for two or three years gradually opening upon my mind. But though I have thus slowly and by degrees obtained light from above to see the Established Church somewhat in her true colours, it is, I confess, only but very lately that the sin of remaining in her has been forcibly laid upon my conscience. I have felt of late that, by continuing one of her ministers, I was upholding what in the sight of the holy Jehovah is hateful and loathsome. I have felt that, by standing up in her pulpit, I was sanctioning a system in principle and practice, in root and branches, corrupt before God. I have felt that I was keeping those children of God who sat under my ministry in total darkness as to the nature of a true Gospel Church. I have felt that both I myself, and the spiritual people that attended my ministry, were, in principle and system, mixed up with the ungodly, the Pharisee, the formalist, the worldling, and the hypocrite. And thus, whilst I remained in the Church of

England, my principles and my practice, my profession and my conduct, my preaching and my acting, were inconsistent with each other. I was building up with the right hand what I was pulling down with the left. I was contending for the power, whilst the Church of England was maintaining the form. I was, by my preaching, separating the people of God from 'the world lying in wickedness', and the Church of England, in her Liturgy and Offices, was huddling together the spiritual and the carnal, the regenerate and the unregenerate, the sheep and the goats. I was contending for regeneration as a super-natural act wrought upon the souls of the elect alone by the Eternal Spirit, and the Church of England was thanking God for regenerating every child that was sprinkled with a little water. True prayer I was representing as the Spirit's work upon the soul, as the groanings of a burdened heart, as the pouring out of a broken spirit, as the cry of a child to his heavenly Father, as the hungering and thirsting of a soul that panted after God. The Church of England tied me down to cold, hackneyed, wearisome forms, in which I prayed for the Royal Family, the Parliament, the Bishops, and all sorts and conditions of men, with scarcely one petition that the Spirit would indite in a regenerate heart. My soul was pained and burdened within me at hearing the wicked and the careless take into their lips the sweet petitions of David in the Psalms. I heard around me those who I knew from their life and conversation had never for a moment spiritually felt the pangs of a wounded conscience, say, 'I stick fast in the deep mire where no ground is; I am come into deep waters, so that the floods run over me'. I heard those who never desired or longed after anything but the gratification of their own lusts and covetousness, repeat aloud, 'Like as the hart desireth the water-brooks, so longeth my soul after thee, O God'. Those that were dressed up in all the colours of the rainbow, I heard saying, 'As for me, I am poor and needy'. Graceless men who had never felt a drop of the Spirit's teachings, and who out of the Church swore, jeered, and scoffed, would cry in my hearing, 'Take not thy Holy Spirit from me'. Adulterers and adulteresses repeated aloud, 'I will wash my hands in innocency, and so will I go to Thine altar'. Whilst the self-righteous Pharisee would sound in my ears, 'I will go forth in the strength of the Lord God, and will make mention of Thy righteousness only'. Thus the gracious and blessed experience of God's saints was mocked and trampled upon, and the fervent prayers and breathings of the Spirit in contrite souls were profaned by the ungodly taking them into their unhallowed lips. And all this I was conscious was not a casual occurrence, or such as arose from the un-suggested will of individuals, but was the deliberate principle and system of the Church of England. I saw it was so by her teaching every child to say he was made in his baptism 'a member of Christ, a child of God, and an inheritor of the kingdom of Heaven'. I saw it was so by that system of responses which she enjoins upon all the congregation to make, and again and again has my soul been burdened at hearing the wicked little children around me mock God by shouting out the responses, as they had been systematically trained to do by ignorant ministers, parents, school-masters and school-mistresses. Being for the last three years a hearer and not a reader of the Liturgy, I have been compelled at times to close my ears with both my hands, that I might not hear the mechanical cries of the children, one of whose responses they always thus worded, 'We have left undone those things which we ought *not* to have done'. I have groaned within me at hearing the ungodly around me thus mock God, and so far was I from joining in the dead and spiritless forms of the Prayer Book, that I could only secretly pray, 'Lord, deliver me from this worldly and unholy system'. Every dull and dry prayer

[187]

seemed to lay a fresh lump of ice on my heart, and when I got into the pulpit, nothing but the hand of God, to whom I cried for help, could take off that deadness and barrenness which these wearisome forms had, in a great measure, laid upon me. At times, too, when I viewed the gettings up and sittings down, the bowings, the turnings to the East, the kneeling in this place and standing in that, and the whole routine of that 'bodily service' wherewith the blessed Jehovah was mocked, I could not but look on the whole as a few degrees only removed from the mummery of a Popish mass-house.

But though I felt, and at times could groan beneath the wretched formality of the Church of England, I was from two motives chiefly kept within her. One was, that I desired to be useful to the children of God in a dark neighbourhood, with whom I had been connected for nearly seven years, and of whom some professed to derive profit from my ministry. The other was altogether carnal, and, though hiding itself in the secret recesses of my heart and therefore unperceived, was doubtless of much weight with me. This was the desire of retaining that independence which my Fellowship secured. My heart, I freely confess, has often sunk within me at the prospect of my already weak health terminating in confirmed illness, with poverty and want staring me in the face. I was also praying for an opening from the Lord to show me my path clearly, as, though I was determined neither to accept preferment, nor take another curacy, I was unwilling to throw up my ministry until the death of the very aged incumbent.[1] Lately, however, I have been brought to see 'that I must not do evil that good may come', and that if my conscience was fully convinced of the sin of remaining in the Church of England, no clearer or more direct intimation of the will of God was needed.

[1] He died in less than six weeks after the resignation of my curacy. [The footnotes to this Letter were added before publication.]

Thus have I laid open the inward workings of my heart, and the experience through which I have been led, in order to show that the resignation of my Fellowship and Curacy, and secession from the Church of England, is no sudden and hasty step, but the gradual and deliberate conviction of my soul.

But besides these particular evils under which I especially 'groaned, being burdened', as being brought into continual contact with them, I have felt that by continuing in the Establishment I sanction and uphold every other corruption that is mixed up with so worldly a system. Thus I must sanction the union of Church and State; the putting of the King in the place of Christ as Head of the Church; the luxury and pomp of the bishops; the giving away of livings for electioneering purposes; the heaping of preferment by ungodly parents on ungodly children; the system of tithes;[1] the principle and practice of Ecclesiastical Courts; the manufacturing of ministers by the gross at the Bishops' ordinations, and all that mass of evil which has sprung out of a worldly and wealthy Establishment. When Christ has bidden me 'call no man Father on earth', and not to be called myself 'Rabbi', and 'Master', and consequently by no title distinctive of priesthood or ministerial office, I must sanction the decking out of

---

[1] I cannot but wonder how men who profess spiritual religion, and call themselves Evangelical ministers, can take tithes from carnal and ungodly farmers; nay, as I have known some do, screw them up to the highest pitch, and even employ legal means to enforce their payment; whilst others of the same name and pretension exact tithes from gardens watered by the sweat of the labourer, and enforce burial and similar fees from the poor, when they themselves ride about in their carriages and phaetons. Of this I am confident, that they are not taught thus to act by the Blessed Spirit, who guides the regenerate into all truth, makes the conscience tender, and gives bowels of compassion towards the poor and needy. The New Testament authorizes no other payment to ministers but free and voluntary offerings; and thus all tithes, fees, and dues are part of that 'mystery of iniquity' of which Babylon, the mother of harlots, is the head.

His professed ministers with the trappings of Antichrist, such proud titles, I mean, as Reverend, Very Reverend, Right Reverend, Most Reverend, Father in God, My Lord, Your Grace, and the like. As a minister of the Establishment I must also sanction that abominable traffic in livings whereby 'the souls of men' are bought and 'sold' (an especial mark of Babylon, Rev. 18:13), and knocked down to the highest bidder by the auctioneer's hammer. Thus the whole system, in its root, stem, and branches, manifests itself to a renewed and spiritual mind as part and parcel of that Antichrist and Babylon which the Lord foreshowed His servants should arise, and from which He calls them to come out and be separate.

As a member, too, of the University, and Fellow of a College, I am unavoidably and necessarily mixed up with many evils, which I am convinced are equally hateful to God. Thus, in this capacity, I must sanction the whole principle of a University, as needful to qualify men to become ministers of Jesus Christ. But who that knows experimentally the sovereignty of Jehovah in choosing His ministers will not feel it to be awful presumption thus to train up unregenerate men to stand forth in His holy name? The call to the ministry is as sovereign as the call by grace. And Jehovah will take the tinker from his barrow, and the cobbler from his stall, and send them to preach His Word, as he took Elisha from the plough, and Amos from 'gathering sycamore fruit'. By continuing, therefore, a member of the University I tacitly set aside the gifts and graces of the Holy Spirit, which can alone qualify a man for the ministry, and substitute a knowledge of Latin and Greek, and such mere letter-learning as is called Divinity. But by doing this I necessarily reject as ministers some of God's most eminent and deeply-taught servants, as Bunyan, Hart, and Huntington; and exalt in their room unregenerate men, who were never taught a single truth by the Eternal Spirit. And as, by continuing a member of the University, I sanction its principle, so in some measure do I sanction its practice. What that practice is, let those testify who have passed through the various stages of Undergraduate, Bachelor, and Master of Arts. But where in all that practice do I see the marks of Christ, or 'the footsteps of His flock'? Can they be traced in the drawing and dining-rooms of the Heads of Houses? in the Common-rooms of the Fellows? in the breakfasts, wine-parties, and suppers of the Undergraduates? What, I would ask, is usually heard in the latter but shouting, and singing of unclean songs, or conversation on the boat-race, the steeple-chase, or the fox-hunt? and what is commonly heard in the former but the news and politics of the day, and all such trifling, and sometimes even unseemly conversation, as is the mark of the soul that is 'dead in sins'? Where amongst all these, either professed ministers of Jesus Christ or such as are training to be so, is the name of the Saviour, or the voice of prayer heard? If anywhere, it is amongst a few despised undergraduates, who have enough religion to see the open evils around them, but not enough grace or faith to separate from the system altogether.

And who that knows the University will not allow the following to be a faint sketch of the course run by most of her children? Initiated in boyhood in wickedness at one of the public schools, those dens of iniquity, or at a private school, in some cases but a shade better and in others worse, the youthful aspirant to the ministry removes to College, where, having run a career of vanity and sin for three years, he obtains his degree. Fortified with this, and his College testimonials, procured without difficulty except by the very notoriously immoral, and those who have shown some symptoms of spiritual religion, he presents himself to the Bishop for ordination. Examined by the Bishop's Chaplain on a few commonplace topics of divinity, and approved, he is ordained amidst a heap of other candidates, without one question of a spiritual nature, one inquiry as to his own conversion to God, or one serious expostulation as to his motives and qualifications for so awful a work. The cold heartlessness and technical formality usually displayed by Bishop, Chaplain, Archdeacon, and Registrar, with the carelessness and levity of most of the candidates, can never be forgotten by one whose heart God has touched, and who has witnessed the solemn mockery of a half-yearly ordination.

But further, as a Fellow of a College, I am connected with a body of men, who, however amiable and learned they may be (and if I forget the kindness of some of them I should be ungrateful indeed), are yet ignorant of Jesus Christ. Their acts as a body I am a party to, and indirectly, if not directly, sanction. Thus I help to give away college livings to unregenerate men, though I may know in my own conscience that they are not even called by grace, much less to the work of the ministry. I am a party also to giving testimonials indiscriminately of good life and conduct to be presented to the Bishop by the candidates for ordination (the document requiring the college seal), as well as to the electing of Fellows and Scholars for their classical attainments, and thus thrusting them into the ministry, and, in a word, to the whole system of education pursued, which, as a means of qualifying men to be ministers, I believe to be hateful to God. In short, I am mixed up with a society of men whose life and conduct, however amiable, moral, and honourable, are not those of 'the poor and afflicted' family of God. No other way, then, have I to escape these evils, to 'keep myself pure, and not to be partaker of other men's sins,' than by fleeing out of Babylon.

Lastly, I secede from the Church of England because I can find in her scarce one mark of a true church. She tramples upon one ordinance of Christ by sprinkling infants, and calling it regeneration (the Word of God allowing no other than the baptism of believers, and that by immersion), and profanes the other by permitting the ungodly to participate. The true Church is despised, but *she* is honoured. The true Church is persecuted, but *she* is a persecutor. The true Church is chosen out of the world, but *she* is part and parcel of it. The true Church consists only of the regenerate, but *she* embraces in her universal arms all the drunkards, liars, thieves, and immoral characters of the land. She christens them, she confirms them, she marries them, she buries them. And she pronounces of all for whom she executes these offices, that they are *regenerate*,[1] that '*all their sins are forgiven them*',[2] that they are '*the servants of God*'.[3] If perchance on a dying bed any doubts and convictions should arise that all is not right for eternity, she sends her minister to visit them, and '*to absolve them from all their sins*'.[4] And having thus lulled their fears, and deluded them to die in peace, she quiets the rising doubts of their friends at the mouth of the grave, by assuring them that 'this our brother is delivered out of the miseries of this sinful world', and is 'committed to the dust in sure and certain hope of the resurrection to eternal life'.[5] Oh! could the awful veil that hides eternity be for a moment lifted up, we should see that thousands, whom the Church of England is blessing, God is cursing, and that tens of thousands whom she is asserting to be 'in joy and felicity', are at that moment 'lifting up their eyes in hell, being in torment'. And while she thus speaks peace and comfort to all that will call her Mother, although unregenerate and dead in sins, she in her canons excommunicates and pronounces 'guilty of wicked error' all that are enlightened of the Spirit to declare she is not a true church, and separate from her communion. What is this but to remove the

[1] Baptismal Service. [2] Confirmation Service. [3] Marriage Service.
[4] See the Popish Form of Absolution in 'The Visitation of the Sick'.
[5] Burial Service.

ancient landmarks of truth and error; 'to call evil good, and good evil; to put darkness for light, and light for darkness, bitter for sweet, and sweet for bitter'? At the same time, she shuts up and seals the mouth of all her ministers, and ties them down to say what she says, and to deny what she denies, by compelling them to 'give their unfeigned assent and consent to all and everything contained and prescribed in and by the Common Prayer Book', and to promise that they will 'conform to the Liturgy as by law established'. And if any of them are haply taught of God the things of Christ in their own souls, and having grace and faithfulness to preach what they have tasted, felt, and handled, contradict in the pulpit what they assert in the desk, they are frowned on by Bishops, despised by the clergy around them, and hated by all the worldly part of their parish, until at length the powerful convictions of an enlightened conscience force them to deliver their souls by fleeing out of Babylon.

But I am told that the Church of England is the only true church; that she derives her sacraments and ministers in a direct, uninterrupted line from the apostles, and that to secede from her is to be guilty of schism. But where are the outward marks of this only true church? Where are the 'signs' of these successors of the apostles, as 'wrought amongst us in all patience, in signs and wonders, and mighty deeds'? (2 Cor. 12:12). Are they to be found in lordly Bishops, proud and pampered dignitaries, fox-hunting, shooting, dancing, and card-playing clergy? Or are they to be discovered in those mere moral and outwardly decent ministers, who, after their solemn vow 'to lay aside the study of the world and the flesh', busy themselves in classics, mathematics, history, modern languages, natural philosophy, divinity, and everything and anything but to know Christ in their own souls? Where are the gifts and graces of the Holy Ghost visible in men, who, not being able to utter a word but what is written down, either copy their sermons from books, or forge out of their own heads a weekly lecture on stale morality? Where are the seals of their commission, whereby they 'approve themselves as ministers of God, by pureness, by knowledge, by kindness, by the Holy Ghost, by love unfeigned, by the word of truth, by the power of God, by the armour of righteousness on the right hand and on the left'? (2 Cor. 6 : 6, 7).

But, perhaps, these outward marks of the successors of the apostles may be discovered in the Evangelical clergy, by some esteemed so highly. What are these, however, as a body, now generally doing but making common cause with the worldly clergy, whom in their hearts they consider to be neither Christians nor ministers, to uphold an unholy system? They are for the most part compounding their sermons out of Simeon's dry and marrowless 'Skeletons',[1] looking out for preferment, buying and selling livings, training up their unregenerate sons for the ministry, and 'putting them into the priest's office that they may eat a piece of bread'. Who amongst them can give a clear and decisive account of his call by grace, or of his call to the ministry? What description can they give of the entrance of the law into their conscience, bringing with it guilt, condemnation, and death, and of a deliverance by the inward revelation of Christ and the application of the 'blood of sprinkling'? The greater part are violently opposed to the fundamental doctrines of unconditional election, particular redemption, imputed righteousness, and man's helplessness. And

---

[1] These said 'Skeletons' of Mr Simeon, of Cambridge, are sketches of sermons from Genesis to Revelation, properly divided and sub-divided, to be filled up according to the ability of the preacher. On these *patent crutches* most of the evangelical ministers walk. But how little the inventor, and the users of such miserable devices, seem to reflect that the Lord 'hates robbery for burnt-offerings', and 'is against those prophets that steal their words every one from his neighbour'!

those who do set forth the doctrines of free and sovereign grace preach them with such dryness and deadness as clearly show that they were never wrought into their experience by the blessed Spirit. Under their ministry the spiritual children of God will not sit; for knowing little or nothing of the work of regeneration, and the trials, temptations, or consolations of the people of Christ, they cannot approve themselves to the consciences of the spiritual, either as called by grace or as sent to preach the gospel.

Thus, with perhaps a few and rare exceptions, the Clergy of the Church of England, whether Orthodox or Evangelical, correspond to that description given by the Holy Ghost, Micah 3:11: 'The heads thereof judge for reward, and the priests thereof teach for hire, and the prophets thereof divine for money, yet will they lean upon the Lord, and say, Is not the Lord among us? none evil can come upon us.' And need we wonder if, as is the priest, so is the people? The congregation of the High church, or *Orthodox* clergy, as they proudly call themselves, consists, with possibly a few exceptions, of none but open sinners, self-righteous pharisees, and dead formalists. In this 'congregation of the dead' the blind lead the blind, and all their weekly confessions, absolutions, prayers, praises, services, and sacraments are, as they will one day find, but one continual mockery of the blessed God, who requires of His worshippers that they 'should worship Him in spirit and in truth'. Of those who sit under the ministry of the Evangelical clergy, the greater part in no wise differ from 'the congregation of the dead' described above, being attracted thither by the superstitious charm of the *Parish Church*. Of the remaining part, there may be a few seeking souls who range over these barren heaths, until fairly driven from them by starvation, or brought off by tasting the green pastures and still waters of gospel grace under an experimental minister. The rest are mere formalists, with an evangelical creed in their heads, but without any grace in their hearts; or, if the minister be a high Calvinist, such 'twice dead' doctrinal professors as never felt the plague of their own hearts, never had their consciences ploughed up by the law, never loathed themselves in their own sight, and were never 'plunged in the ditch till their own clothes abhorred them'. Humble, lowly, contrite souls, who are deeply acquainted with the workings of grace and of corruption, whose consciences have been made tender, and who have landmarks of the dealings of God with them, cannot long continue where they have fellowship with neither minister nor people. And, indeed, so opposed is the whole principle and practice of the Church of England to the work of grace upon the souls of the elect, and 'to simplicity and godly sincerity', that a minister, who is not a hypocrite or a formalist, must, when he has reached a certain point in Christian experience, either flee out of her or awfully sin against the convictions of his own conscience. He may remain in her as a presumptuous dead Calvinist; he may take the highest tone of doctrine, and preach Sunday after Sunday about assurance of personal salvation; but if once he describe the work of the Spirit on the soul he must, at a certain point, either come out of her or, by remaining contentedly within her pale, manifest himself a hypocrite in experience, of all hypocrites and of all hypocrisies the most deceiving and the most awful. Can a man, for instance, who has known the work of regeneration in his own soul, and whose conscience is made tender by the blessed Spirit, go on long to lie unto God by thanking Him for regenerating infants? Can he who has been sprinkled with the blood of Christ, and been fed with His flesh, continue long to give the elements of His body and blood to the unbeliever, the self-righteous, and the ungodly? Can he who has tasted the covenant of grace, and experimentally entered into the everlasting distinction between the sheep and the goats, go on long to mock God by declaring at the grave's mouth of every departed unbeliever, swearer, and drunkard, that he is a 'brother', and is 'taken to be with God'? Notions in the head, however correct, doctrines, however high, a presumptuous confidence of salvation, however loud and lofty, may suffer a man thus to trifle with the living JEHOVAH. But a tender conscience, a godly fear, and a trembling sense of God's holiness and majesty, such as the blessed Spirit works in the soul, must sooner or later bring a man out of this awful mockery.

From this worldly and unholy system I now secede; and blessed be the name of God Most High, who has poured light on my eyes to see these abominations, and given me, I trust, a small portion of that faith of Moses whereby 'he was willing rather to suffer affliction with the people of God, than to enjoy the pleasures of sin for a season'. For sooner far would I die in a workhouse, under the sweet shinings-in of the eternal Comforter, and His testimony to my conscience that I am born of God, than live and die in ease and independence, without following Jesus in that path of trial and suffering which alone leads to eternal life.

But my long relationship with yourself, as Head of Worcester College, and with my brother Fellows, will not allow me thus to dissolve my connexion with you without faithfully warning both you and them of your present state before God. What marks, then, are there in you, or them, of that new birth, without which none can enter the kingdom of heaven? What signs have you, or they, of a broken and contrite spirit? What marks of 'the faith of God's elect'? What inward discoveries have you, or they, had of the blood and righteousness of Christ? What testimony of the blessed Spirit to the pardon of your sins, and to your adoption into the family of God? 'If any man have not the Spirit of Christ, he is none of His', though a sound classic, an acute mathematician, or a learned divine. And to have been professed ministers of Jesus Christ will only add to your condemnation, if you and they live and die in your present state of unbelief and unregeneracy.

I am weak and ignorant, full of sin and compassed with infirmity, but I bless God that He has in some measure shown me the power of eternal things, and by free and sovereign grace stopped me in that career of vanity and sin in which, to all outward appearance, I was fast hurrying down to the chambers of death.

With all due respect to you as Provost of Worcester College, I beg leave to subscribe myself,

Yours faithfully,

J. C. PHILPOT

Index

The Aged Pilgrims' Friend Society

THIS REVISED EDITION OF 'THE SECEDERS' HAS been produced with the co-operation of The Aged Pilgrims' Friend Society who have for a number of years been solely responsible for the sale and circulation of the larger two-volume edition (published in 1930–32) copies of which are still available from the Society in attractive binding, 15s. for both volumes, post free.

The fact that Dr J. H. Philpot had expressed the wish that at his death the profits from the existing stock of his father's biography should go to a Society concerned with helping elderly Christians needs some explanation and the present publishers are happy to supply it in the following notes.

J. C. Philpot was one of the many spiritual leaders of the last century to commend the work of the Aged Pilgrims' Friend Society, not only for the practical good which it did, but also for the spirit of Christian love and loyalty to Calvinistic theology which it exhibited. In the sweeping religious changes which have taken place in the present century this Society continued to stand by the Faith which had led to its existence and consequently Dr Philpot donated his work to what he called his father's 'pet charity'.

The Aged Pilgrims' Friend Society had its origins in the wave of practical blessings which followed the great eighteenth-century revival in England. It was founded in 1807 by James Bisset and a small group of young Sunday school teachers connected with Whitefield's Tabernacle, Moorfields, London. At a time when large numbers of the working classes were being literally pauperized and the administration of the Poor Law had completely broken down, their object was to give financial assistance to aged and poor members of the household of faith in the form of small life pensions of £5 5s. per annum. During the first year just over £18 was collected, and the first three pensioners elected.

Among its earliest subscribers was the honoured name of William Wilberforce, and not a few of the first Christians to benefit from the Society had sat under the ministry of men like George Whitefield, William Romaine, Daniel Rowlands, John Newton and William Huntington. Later in the century such evangelical leaders as C. H. Spurgeon were prominent in their support of the work and Spurgeon preached for the Society on several occasions.

After the evident blessing which rested on the small beginnings of the Society, the possibility of doing further service to Christ by providing homes for aged believers was realized. Thus besides giving financial help to pensioners the first Home was opened at Camberwell in 1834, accommodating forty-two pilgrims. A second and larger Home was opened at Hornsey Rise in 1871 and today the Society has nine Homes and four Nursing Sections, ministering to over 200 of the Lord's people. Each resident has his or her own bed-sitting room and kitchenette, and lives a free and independent life. In these ways the Society has been enabled to care for over 13,000 who in the eventide of life have needed and appreciated Christian fellowship and practical brotherly love.

It is the publishers' wish that as this book revives the largely forgotten memory of two spiritual men, it might also draw the attention of a wider number of Christians today to the work of the Society in which they were so closely interested. Although the coming of the Welfare State has in some ways altered the forms of assistance needed by the elderly there remains much that the State can never do. The Aged

Pilgrims' Friend Society began in spiritually brighter times than these and in days when its doctrinal convictions would command far more sympathy than they receive from much contemporary Christianity.

The Banner of Truth Trust is glad to be associated by the present reprint with the Aged Pilgrims' Friend Society and we commend its ministry to the interest and support of our readers. Further information and literature can be obtained from The Secretary, Aged Pilgrims' Friend Society, 19 Ludgate Hill, London, E.C.4.

'Blessed is he that considereth the poor: the Lord will deliver him in time of trouble. The Lord will preserve him, and keep him alive; and he shall be blessed upon the earth: and thou wilt not deliver him unto the will of his enemies. The Lord will strengthen him upon the bed of languishing: thou wilt make all his bed in his sickness.' Psalm 41 : 1–3.

Some other Banner of Truth Trust titles:

Biographical:

The Early Years	C. H. Spurgeon	21/–
Men of the Covenant	Alexander Smellie	21/–
Five English Reformers	J. C. Ryle	2/6
Five Christian Leaders	J. C. Ryle	4/6
Andrew Bonar—Diary and Life		15/–
The Life of Robert Murray M'Cheyne	Andrew Bonar	3/6

Doctrinal:

The Doctrine of the Holy Spirit	George Smeaton	15/–
The Confession of Faith	A. A. Hodge	13/6
The Sovereignty of God	A. W. Pink	2/6
The Work of the Holy Spirit	Octavius Winslow	3/–
The Doctrine of Justification	James Buchanan	21/–
The Church of Christ (2 vols)	James Bannerman	30/–

Puritan Works:

A Lifting Up for the Downcast	William Bridge	5/–
Heaven on Earth	Thomas Brooks	5/–
The Death of Death	John Owen	15/–
The Ten Commandments	Thomas Watson	8/–

Bible Commentaries:

Commentary on the Holy Bible—3 Volumes	Matthew Poole	per vol. 42/–
Psalms	David Dickson	21/–
The Epistle to the Hebrews	John Brown	21/–

General Works:

An All Round Ministry	C. H. Spurgeon	10/6
Letters of John Newton		2/6

For free illustrated catalogue write to:

THE BANNER OF TRUTH TRUST
78B Chiltern Street, London, W.1